IF THIS BE LOVE

IF THIS BE LOVE

Mohinder Singh

KALPAZ

If This Be Love

ISBN : 978-81-7835-945-8

Published 2013 in India by
Kalpaz Publications
C-30, Satyawati Nagar,
Delhi - 110052
E-mail: kalpaz@hotmail.com
Ph. 9212729499

Laser Type Setting : Sanya Computers, Delhi
Printed at : Chawla Offset Printers, Delhi

Contents

Contents

Part-I

Part-I

1 The Tragedy at Polo Play

It was a typical December day in Jaipur. The glorious sun-warmed afternoon was enlivened by a light cool breeze. Last night's short shower did settle the dust, imparting a sparkle to the air. Pretty puffs of white clouds floated in the deep blue sky. You saw kites—the sovereigns of the sky—flying high overhead, circling lazily yet ever alert to the chance to pounce on a meaty morsel on the ground.

A polo match was in progress at the Rambagh Palace ground, the acclaimed polo field that had been the venue of many a memorable contest since its formation in the fifties. The Duke of Edinburgh played here and so also game legends like Rao Raja Hanut Singh. It had even seen polo being played on the backs of elephants and on bikes.

The smooth grassy stretch was only 200/160 yards. This was against the standard polo field of 300/200 yards, with supporting side-boards during match play. Yet, the location is picturesque and the surroundings superb. Ample safety zone is provided behind the flexible goal posts and the touch lines. In off-polo time, the ground doubled up as a fairway for three holes of the adjacent golf course. The arrangement was said to be temporary till the golf club developed its own regular course.

The day's fixture was between the local-based 61st Cavalry (the only fighting regiment in the world keeping its horses, more for polo and parades) led by Major Udai Singh, and a select Rajput chieftains' team (the Daredevils) put together and captained by Sarabjeet Singh Rathore, popularly going by the name "Bwana".

Sarabjeet had once taken a polo team to South Africa. On the way back, they had a makeshift polo fixture at the port of Mombassa, Kenya. There, everyone from room boys and taxi drivers to hotel managers and local dignitaries addressed him as Bwana, the Swahili equivalent of boss or chief. Swahili language is a mixture of Arabic and local dialect, mainly derived from the Arabic culture in the area. Sarabjeet was even presented with an Arab regalia, an elegant long shirt with a matching head scarf. A photograph showing him wearing that dress would adorn his living room. Sarabjeet's imposing presence at six feet one with broad shoulders and a masterly expression had evoked such a response.

The term caught on with Sarabjeet's teammates, and also with others back home—a fitting address for the tall, handsome, muscular Rajput chief. The wide forehead, thick eyebrows, long nose, and striking moustache endowed him with an aura of authority, a well-nigh princely bearing. What attracted one most about him were his deep brown eyes. You always found him immaculately dressed in western clothes or embroidered silk kurta-pajama, unless he was in his riding outfit.

Scores of polo celebrities and former stalwarts of the game were seated on cushioned cane chairs ranged along the clubhouse. You could spot quite a few chieftains of the former princely states, with their ancient Bentleys and Rolls-Royces kept shining in the parking lot. Tea, coffee, and cakes were on offer. The gathering was brightened by a bevy of pretty women, daintily dressed. And this included the glamorous Maharani of Jaipur, clad in a pink chiffon sari. Most invitees were having a pullover handy, expecting it to get chilly around sunset.

You had the Cavalry band in attendance. The polo trophy was there on a table beside the big clock. This trophy was a huge silver goblet. In celebration the winning team was apt to press it into use for quaffing champagne.

The city's polo fans, and these could be counted in hundreds, had taken positions atop the long, stone boundary wall by the roadside. Watching a polo match involves no entry fee. And a good polo match is always exciting to see; the sheer speed of the game, the thud of horses' hooves, the shouts of players, the tussle between sweating mounts, the clanking of mallets, the slaps of whips sending horses into bursts of speed, quick turns with riders keeping their weight on the inside, and the plastic ball flying fast.

It was a knowledgeable, well-behaved city crowd consisting almost entirely of males. Like golf spectators, the polo viewers appreciated and applauded every good play irrespective of the side they backed. The vocal support appeared equally divided for the Cavalry (red shirts) and the Daredevils (green shirts). Muslims seemed to be in a majority. They are said to have a better feel for horses. The assumption may well have something in it; most tonga-drivers are Muslims.

On one boundary side were ranged strings of relief ponies with protective boots strapped to lower legs and fetlocks, manes shaved off and tails tied. The feisty animals tramped impatiently, held by their syces. Standing nearby, you were assailed by the smell of horses and of their droppings.

The 61st Cavalry had most of its horses imported from Australia. These were generally big in size and made a good showing at ceremonials and parades. The Cavalry bosses have picked out around fifty ponies for polo play and trained them accordingly. Major Udai Singh was mainly responsible for picking up the Cavalry team and the horses. He himself was particularly fond of the horse that went by the name "Bully". It was an apt name because the horse was high strung, almost domineering. Udai often rode Bully in the crucial last *chukka*.

The two mounted umpires, themselves noted polo players, were at their job and so also the referee seated on the sideline.

Dubbed as a "friendly" match on New Year's Eve, it was turning into an exceptionally tough contest. The helmeted four-member teams, both carrying an equal handicap of 14, stood level at eight goals each after the five seven-minute *chukkas*. Whereas the Cavalry had an edge in scoring field goals, the Daredevils fared better at converting penalty hits into goals. At forty yards Sarabjeet has grown deadly accurate in a penalty shoot out as he would stand still in his stirrups for the shot. He had been putting in umpteen hours of practice on a wooden horse installed at his farm.

With the score even at five *chukkas*, tension arose to a fever pitch in the last one. Early on, the Chieftains' side scored a brilliant goal through a great under-the-neck pass from Sarabjeet (playing at 4) to Ajit at No. 1. The red flag went up signaling a goal. The same sent the Cavalry men into frenzy to equalize, if not win. Tempers were getting high. Even a few obscenities flew across.

With the teams changing sides after the goal, Udai (with the best team handicap of +3 and playing quarterback) made a spectacular run on Bully. Unlike Sarabjeet, a team man, Udai was more of a loner, but a wizard at ball control coupled with bursts of speed. And he would have scored but for a tough tackle by Bwana (handicap +4) who was marking Udai, the Cavalry's best player.

In this riding-off—deemed falling within the right-of-the-way rule that allowed a tackle up to an angle of 45 degrees—a terrible tragedy ensued. As the two snorting, sweaty mounts (Udai's Bully, the newly polo-trained big black Australian pony, and Rani, the smallish sleek grey, lion-hearted Argentinean mare of Bwana, his favourite, and invariably ridden for the crucial 6th *chukka*), jostled violently and stumbled. Both the riders were thrown off. Udai, to the watchers' horror, landed on his head and Bwana, on his back.

In the collision and the fall, Rani, the valiant mare, had badly broken her right front leg. This meant putting it out, shooting it dead, with burial at the farm.

Time of accident: 3:57.

The match was cancelled forthwith. It was no minor accident calling for injury time. The injured were rushed to the nearby Sawai Mansingh Hospital in the attending ambulance. Udai's wife Raminder followed closely a car. In the emergency ward, the injured Udai was hanging between life and death. He appeared to have broken his neck. Bwana lay along side writhing in pain for his crushed back.

Forthwith, the two were moved into the ICU. Udai was connected to various life saving machines, while Bwana was injected pain relieving drugs. Yet it soon became apparent that Udai could not be saved; he had broken his neck. His wife, Raminder, was called in. As Udai lay dying, he could only murmur, "Bwana, look after Rammi." And he was dead. Raminder, lying over him, let out a loud shreik. And then she began to cry. In one afternoon, her world had tumbled. Her life of love and comfort had suddenly turned into one of misery and loneliness.

On the other bed, Bwana was thrashing in pain. The Doctors said, "He has broken his back."

It is no consolation that polo has its share of fatalities. Qutubuddin Aibak, the founder of the Slave Dynasty, died playing the game, and so also Nawab Iftikhar Ali Khan, father of the cricketer Tiger Pataudi. Sawai Mansingh, the erstwhile Jaipur ruler who had put in the Rambagh ground, suffered a head blow in play. He succumbed to his injuries the next day while umpiring a polo match.

You need guts to play polo. The present-day game was started by the British tea planters in Assam. The tough game was mostly taken up by the army and later the Indian chiefs. The rules of the game were laid down by the Hurlingham Club in England.

The planned festivities connected with the New Year's Eve match were called off. The play had turned out far too badly.

2 Bwana's Broken Back

Udai was dead, dead before his 38th birthday, falling on January 18, 1985. He left behind a 34-year-old widow and an 11-year-old daughter.

For Bwana, it was an incapacitating injury to his back.

In Udai's death he had lost his best friend. The two had been buddies for years. Both belonged to landed gentry and were together at Mayo College, Ajmer. They had become close friends. Both excelled in riding while staying mediocre at studies. Later, Udai joined the army while Sarabjeet began his own business. Yet they had developed a deep friendship and left no opportunity to be together.

Sarabjeet also happened to be in love with Raminder, Udai's wife.

Bwana would never be able to forgive himself for the field tackle that resulted in the death of his buddy and rendered his ladylove a widow and the daughter fatherless. What if one could turn the clock back on that tragic polo match!

Now, his time was occupied with attending to his own injuries where pain was a constant companion. He sought relief with morphine and codeine, while it was Valium to sleep at night. The recommended spinal surgery in London had to wait till urgent matters pertaining to Udai's demise were dealt with.

The firewood cremation was carried out with full military honours. Several high-ranking army officers had come to attend. Of course, Raminder's father, a lieutenant general at the army headquarters, was a prominent presence. Much of the city's top strata were there.

Sarabjeet, who himself was being helped to walk, found the widow well-nigh inconsolable. His friend's dying assurance to her that he would always be there with Raminder hardly registered with her. She didn't cry or utter a word. She just sat, numbed.

The suddenness of Udai's death left her shattered. She couldn't comprehend how someone so full of life and vitality would be dead within minutes. She harboured hardly any recollection of the actual accident and the run to the hospital, except for a urine leak in her trousers. Uncontrolable fear. Her response to his death was still shock, even disbelief. At times she blamed herself for not dissuading Udai to play that day. At breakfast Udai had mentioned he wasn't feeling on top of the world—maybe it was a premonition of the coming tragedy. And she had seen him downing two large gin at the lunch get-together, his way of pepping himself up for the contest.

"You're getting a bit out of shape, putting on weight," she had been telling him lately. "Better reduce alcohol intake and step up strenuous exercise."

"Sure. That's exactly my resolution for the coming year."

For some time, Raminder had been unhappy over the amount of drinks Udai was taking. She had even communicated her unease over it to Bwana. One late evening when everybody had gone away at Bwana's dinner, the only ones remaining were Udai, Raminder and the host. While Bwana and Raminder were sipping their coffee, Udai got up and poured for himself half a glass of Napolean brandy. He had already taken three stiff whiskies before his dinner. Bwana noticed a pained expression on Raminder's face. Seeing this, he ventured out, "The US Surgeon General advises no more than twenty-one drinks for a man in a week, and fourteen for a woman." Udai, who had swallowed a big gulf of brandy, shot back, "Fuck the Surgeon General." He, then added, "Funny, how you could be a surgeon and a general at the same time?" The joke evoked a mild titter in his listeners.

Simran, the lanky lass, kept on crying almost non-stop. At the cremation, with Udai's younger brother, Davinder, setting the bier alight, her loud wails wrung the hearts of those around.

Bwana underwent prolonged spinal surgery at London's Princess Grace Hospital Spinal Centre. He was accompanied by his friend Dr. Adoor, a spinal surgeon at Swai Mansingh Hospital. The squashed discs at the lower end of the vertebra were removed and replaced by plastic ones, aided by synthetic cushioning material. He needed a few other metal supports at the upper end of the vertebra. And he had to wear a heavy brace around his neck. The operating senior surgeon, a relatively youngish-looking doctor with serious expression and skillful hand, told Sarabjeet, "You are out of danger but I'm not sure whether you will ever walk again. Anyway you'd require a prolonged stay at a rehabilitation centre before a final word can be said about your legs." Sarabjeet was just lost for words.

Thereafter, a year of rehabilitation followed at a Surrey rehab clinic. This was an impressive complex located in the countryside, surrounded by forest and a narrow river in front. The odd fifty–sixty inmates were all with serious disabilities, such as no use of legs or a missing arm. Yet, to Bwana, most of them appeared fairly cheerful.

The routine of the rehab centre was rigorous, continuing from nine in the morning till six in the evening. Bwana's roommate, a man around thirty, moved in a wheelchair and had become quite proficient in the use of it. To some extent, he helped Bwana in lifting his low spirits, told him that an acceptable sort of life could be managed with a wheelchair. However, Bwana sometimes got so depressed with the prospects of never walking on his own that he even contemplated suicide. But then, he thought of his twin daughters and, as always, Raminder.

Every day Bwana underwent hours of physiotherapy. Two stout Irish nurses took turns moving his legs up and down, making him walk with their support, and helped him do endless other exercises on machines.

When Bwana was in the rehab centre, Shanti used to visit him at least once a week. The married daughter living in Oxford was in an advanced stage of pregnancy. Dr. Nari, her husband and younger brother of Dr. Adoor, was too busy at his London eye clinic to make it more than once in a month. Kranti, who was in the US, came on a short visit. Rammi rang him quite often but she expressed her helplessness in not being able to come to see him, though she dearly wished him well.

A year passed and Bwana was still at the rehab centre. It was time to have a talk with the head man as to whether it would be useful to stay on any longer or go back home. Mr. Sinclair, the institute's director was a thin, tall man with greying hair and a prominent nose, came to see him one afternoon.

"You have been an ideal trainee. And we have done all that we could do for you. As far as we are concerned, you can go back to your country."

"Will I ever walk? Or I have to spend the rest of my life in a wheelchair. I hate moving in a wheelchair."

"I appreciate your point of view. Yet I'm not sure whether you would ever be able to walk firmly. Your legs have grown too weak because of the back injury. However, they have some sensation in them. Well, with a bit of luck you may be able to walk indoors. Till then you will have to take the help of a walker or crutches in the house. For any outside movement over a length of time, there seems no escape from a wheelchair. To undergo this disability at forty-two, I know it would be particularly hard on you—a fine polo player, good rider, tennis player, golfer ..."

"At times, I wish I had died in the same polo accident where my friend perished."

"Well, life has compensations. You may come to enjoy some altered lifestyle, read more, play chess and cards, write something. For exercise, you can do as much swimming as you like. Swimming is the best exercise for your back. And take more interest in your family and friends."

"Please be frank with me. Will I recover my manhood?"

"It will take time, but I see no reason why you should not recover your sexual power. But what you will require is a loving woman who would patiently and endearingly invoke your sexual rejuvenation."

"You know I've no wife, and paid women have no patience in such a situation."

"Better marry someone who would love you. You're still young and handsome, and I assume rich enough to support a wife."

"This last assumption of yours is not wrong," he agreed, with some slight satisfaction.

Mr. Sinclair eased himself into a chair near Bwana's bed side as if prepared for a longish talk. "Mr. Franklin Roosevelt, the US president, was struck by polio at the age of thirty-nine and lost the use of his legs. Even with steel braces and crutches he could only walk awkwardly. Do you know that in this physical state he electioneered for governorship of New York, then vice presidency, and lastly for presidency. He is the only one who was elected four times as president of the US, because he pulled the country out of the Great Depression with his New Deal social economic measures and sucessfully added America's efforts to the Second World

War, defeating Germany. And mind you, despite his physical handicap, he managed an active love life. Lucy Page Mercer Rutherfurd, his wife Eleanor's former secretary, and Marguerite LeHand were his mistresses.

"Of course, he was helped by a highly energetic and supportive wife. He himself, through swimming and other exercises, had built a muscular upper body that could stand the strain of traveling and long working hours.

"I suggest you read a couple of books on the life of Roosevelt. This will give you strength to cope with your disability. And if you can get that supportive wife, so much the better."

Bwana mumbled that he would do the suggested reading.

Mr. Sinclair shook hands and told Bwana that his assistant would give him written instructions regarding the use of a wheelchair and a list of his medicines.

"Sir, if you ever happen to come to India, you are most welcome to stay as my guest at Jaipur. You would like that city."

"Thanks. I'll keep it in mind."

On return to Devi House, Bwana got a lift installed to the first floor for his bedroom. Ramps were provided on various entrance stairs. He also ordered from London two aluminum wheelchairs, one of them motorized. The new Nissan car had an arrangement where the wheelchair could be rolled into it. Even the lighting in various passages and corridors of the house were brightened.

Seeing Bwana in a wheelchair, Raminder felt very sad. Here was a powerful athletic man reduced to a helpless state of movement. Yet she was keen to cheer him up. For her, he was still the same man whom she had admired for years.

"Your physical condition now calls for a major change in lifestyle, a new sort of living. One hopes you don't turn into an entirely different entity!"

"Don't think so. My heart is in the same place."

"You'd have to find new interests, new ways to spend your time. What about taking to bridge?"

"There would be so many things to do," he said half-convinced. Yet he was sure that the life he had loved living was gone for good. No polo, no horse riding, no golf, no tennis and no free movement. To some extent, it will always remain for him a somewhat joyless existence. How a fateful accident had so diminished his life!

On top, he had to look after Raminder, Simran, Shanti, Nargis and Kranti.

3 An Evening Out

A friendship between a widower and a bachelor could wilt with the bachelor's getting married. Here, Bwana the widower had the additional complication of bringing up twin daughters.

This didn't happen between Sarabjeet and Udai. Indeed, Raminder's presence was proving a potent plus factor.

Sarabjeet and Udai had been buddies before Udai married. They were at school together, played polo together, were visiting each other quite often, and met at parties. They had come to like each other a lot. Udai belonged to a prominent Rathore family of Jodhpur. And he had been an officer with the 61st Cavalry stationed at Jaipur. A handsome, barrel-chested 5 feet 10, he was tending to be plump, a consequence of his fondness for food and alcohol. You sometimes saw him picking a savoury from another's plate. What enlivened his face most were a pair of black searching eyes under long eyelashes. The only blemish showing was a scar under the right cheek, arising out of an injury sustained in polo. Udai cut a dashing figure in a neat army uniform or choice civilian clothes. He sported a well trimmed moustache and was always wearing expensive Italian shoes, mirror-shined. Udai looked best in jodhpurs astride his favourite, Bully.

The best thing about Udai was his geniality. He would come up with witty remarks and had a fund of jokes, quite a few ribald. It was always a pleasure being in his company, more so in the evening with drinks flowing freely.

In a way, Bwana had acquired a new family in Raminder and her daughter Simran, let alone Udai. He showered gifts on them; some as expensive as a set of gold Rolex watches and a dinner-cum-tea set of Noritaki china for twelve. He extended no end of hospitality to them and in many other ways he had endeared himself to all the three.

Over the years Sarabjeet was drawn deeper and deeper into affection for the attractive Sikh lady.

Here was Bwana's side of the story:

From the moment I set my eyes on Rammi, I experienced a peculiar pull. Not that I hadn't met pretty women before but she was indeed glamorous. Glamour, I suppose, is something innate which bestows on its lucky possessor charm and charisma. It's something independent of the beauty of a face or the softness of skin.

She was someone you'd notice forthwith among women gathered in a room. Rammi's glamour made her an eye-turner, induced people to seek her company. And Rammi obliged by being an apt listener—men happen to like women who listen well.

Rammi wasn't only popular with menfolk, she was also on friendly terms with most of the ladies. She was good in organizing women's get-togethers and other social events. Even those women who were critical of the supposed extramarital affair they believed she was having with me persuade themselves to participate in Raminder's social parleys.

A slender five feet six, she had an athletic body, a body exuding its own confidence, and sexy, too. She had a body somewhat different from the classical idea of the female form with its emphasis on curves. Yet it stayed appealing.

She was a bit dusky for a Punjabi but oozing oomph. Luxuriant black hair coming down to the hips like a waterfall; hair that had known no clipping. Bold piercing eyes, high shapely breasts, neither too big nor too small, and lascivious lips. She usually wore a sleeveless blouse with arms showing. Who can resist the beauty of a comely woman bare-armed!

When she rode in her tight jeans you couldn't fail to notice the long, slender legs, a couple of inches longer than the average for her height. Yet her most captivating feature was the ready smile. When she smiled—and she smiled a lot—it made her eyes twinkle, cheeks develop bewitching dimples and two rows of pearly teeth showed up.

I had never seen a lady smiling so beautifully. And her smile could say different things on different occasions. It could be an innocent, shy smile, a smile of recognition, a nervous smile, and a totally different smile when she was being flattered.

And what a hearty laugh she gave when you came up with a good joke, even a man's joke.

It was always fun being in her company, watching her, bantering with her, sitting at meals with her, riding together with her, and sharing a host of other activities.

Unlike some other ladies who dressed themselves in gaudy clothes and used too much make-up, Raminder was always in a simple elegant dress that showed taste. At parties and other functions she wore a sari but at home you often saw her in a nicely fitted salwar-kameez. Her make-up was unobtrusive. You often saw her wearing dainty earrings and a chain necklace.

It became almost my daily routine to meet the couple at my place or at theirs. I must surely be their most frequent visitor. And they were automatically invited to every social get-together put on by me.

Indeed, my every day was enlivened in anticipation of meeting her towards the evening.

I enjoyed the company of Udai, too. He was ever welcoming, witty, and sociable. His knowledge about horses and polo was astounding. Even the origin of the word "polo" I learnt from him—the Tibetan word *pulu* for a willow from which the playing balls were made. British tea planters in Assam, the first Englishmen to take to the game, named it "polo"

The horse, he told me, has changed human history more than any other domestic animal. It revolutionized warfare right from Genghis Khan to Alexander to Napoleon. And for centuries till the onset of railways, the speed at which the human being could travel was the speed of the horse.

Udai, I assumed, had high regard for me. He showed no signs of jealousy or unease at my meeting Rammi—maybe he was secure in the belief she loved him and would never betray him. And this belief might well be sound. In turn, Udai was known to be a one-woman man, though polo players do exercise a certain fascination for women. His only weakness, as far as I knew, was alcohol and a propensity to drive cars fast; something he did when he borrowed my Mercedes or BMW.

Late one evening he wanted me to do drugs with him. "Just a snort," he said, "Someone has given me a gram of good-quality cocaine." I declined; I didn't want to lose control of my brain cells, even momentarily.

Yet I had become fairly comfortable with Udai smoking cigarettes or a cigar.

Since I've known Rammi, hundreds of hours have been spent in her company—at times, only the two of us. Yet I haven't kissed her or touched her body in any overt sexual way. At best it has been the customary hug or a parting peck on the cheek or a friendly holding of hands.

As love between a vigorous male and a pretty female goes, ours may be the purest form imaginable. The same, however, has enriched my life, added zest to it. I imagine I had developed an innocent crush on Rammi as if there is a thing like innocent crush.

I am no wife stealer. Yet people don't stop from saying all sorts of things. People evidently assume I sleep with her. People tend to be such experts about things they aren't privy to. Maybe, people think Udai isn't that good in bed—from sitting too long on horseback with the genitals pressed. But then I've been sitting longer on horses.

The familiarity between me and Rammi, I suppose, is the talk of the town, with gossip mills working overtime. Many of my relatives were critical of it; quite a few from selfish reasons that my largesse flowing to Rammi should instead get diverted their way. Some near ones didn't even hesitate to ventilate their misgivings in my presence. Kranti was clearly emerging as the most vociferous of the lot.

Happily, many of my friends looked at this relationship with amused tolerance. Only a few detractors were gloating over what they considered a first-rate scandal.

An army officer, friendly to Udai, and inclined to flirt with Rammi—rating her an easy picking because of her entanglement with me—was prepared to broach the matter directly with Udai in a bid to warn him about me. Good sense prevailed; he was dissuaded from doing so by a saner colleague.

Anyway Udai couldn't be completely in the dark about such rumblings. But he didn't seem to exhibit any signs of discomfort. He maintained the same friendly, open interface with me. He didn't in any manner frown upon my growing association with his wife.

Once Rammi was travelling to Udaipur by the night train, named Chetak (after the famous horse of Maharana Pratap), to attend an NGO meeting for widows' welfare. She was the vice president of the Jaipur

Widows' Welfare branch, with the chief minister's wife as the president. Yet most of the meetings were conducted by Raminder in the absence of the chief minister's wife.

Raminder used to show her distress at the way Hindu society treated widows. They were maligned for the death of their husbands and given almost subhuman treatment after the husband's death. (Who knew that she herself would be a widow for years?)

Simran had to be left back so as not to miss her schooling. My plan at the same time was to travel to Udaipur by air to collect some pending funds from an industrialist who had bought land from me in Gurgaon. Thereafter, my plan was to go to Pune for a few days. Udai persuaded me to travel by train to accompany Rammi.

Early next morning she met me at Udaipur Railway Station by two members of the local NGO. Along with the other delegates, she was also to be put up in a three-star hotel-cum-meeting venue.

A car from the Lake Palace Hotel was waiting for me. This was a very picturesque hotel, a former palace in the middle of the Pichola Lake.

We had discussed in the train that I would have her picked up in the evening when the meeting was over.

Mine had turned into a successful day in the sense that the industrialist concerned paid me the pending dues. After lunch, I had a good sleep for two hours, enjoyed a leisurely bath, and then sent a car to have Raminder picked up.

"Such a wondrous place," Rammi remarked as she entered my room. A short boat ride had brought her to the hotel.

"The marbled rooms make such a perfect setting for the wonderful paintings here. And the location is out of this world."

"I had a tiresome time today. We haggled over the shortage of funds and low level of our activities."

"Why don't you have a tub bath, freshen up, and then we go for a boat ride."

"Not a bad idea."

Raminder came out glowing after half an hour.

"You look most charming," I said and led her by hand to the waiting boat; a small motorized one.

For her it was a first visit to Udaipur, the "City of Lakes". She found it fascinating. By this time it was dusk and lights came on in the palace and various buildings around the lake.

"What a glorious sight!" she exclaimed.

On return, we had a leisurely dinner on an open terrace. She was persuaded to take a glass of red wine while I took a stiff scotch.

"Oh!" she said suddenly, "It's nearly 11 o'clock. I must return to my place; otherwise the gossip-mongers would have a field day."

So it was a boat ride back and from the landing site, I drove her in a rented Toyota to her hotel.

"This is one of the happiest evenings of my life," I said holding her hand, a perfect hand.

"Your coming into our life has been one in the best things that have happened to us. Every one loves you—Udai, Simran, and of course myself."

"I prize your friendship the most. You have enlivened my life, otherwise a dull life."

The departing was a hug and she drew up to give a peck on my cheek.

I was loath to let her go, yet go she must.

She was leaving the next day back to Jaipur by the morning train, giving me no opportunity to be with her one more evening.

Later when Udai died in the horrible polo accident while playing with me, some malicious tongues began to wag that I had killed him purposely to get at his wife. But in circles knowledgeable about polo, this could never pass muster. And in time such talk died out.

4 The Kiss

Here I have to make a confession, mused Bwana. My love of Rammi hasn't been totally devoid of sexual play. An incident did take place, a single incident, an ecstatic, unforgettable incident.

In July 1984, I led an All-India polo team to UK for the Cowdray Gold Cup. We did beat a team from Wales but lost all the other four fixtures. To some extent we suffered the handicap of not having our own ponies—carting ponies to England worked out to be too expensive. I particularly missed Rani, my gallant grey mare.

Our last unofficial match was at Richmond Park against the British Lancers. Udai was the star player and we won by a margin of six goals.

Rammi and Simran had accompanied Udai. She herself played in a women's polo event.

By this time, I had purchased a house on Victoria Road, a rambling stone house with a nicely kept back garden. And this started the practice of living in London during the polo season from July to September.

Udai and his family were staying with me. They were scheduled to leave on August 17. Udai received a call from Delhi to be back by August 13 in connection with duty at Rashtrapati Bhavan on Independence Day.

"Sorry, I'll be missing Rammi's birthday," he said.

Rammi has the luck to be born on August 15, the date of our country's independence. "My father toyed with the idea of naming me Azad Kaur. Mercifully, he was overruled by Mom," Rammi jokes about it. My mother had retorted, "No man would want to marry a woman who was named Azad."

"We'll miss you. But be assured, it'll be duly celebrated," I promised Udai.

How it actually turned out, Udai wouldn't suspect or know.

At breakfast on 15th morning, I presented Rammi a bouquet of twenty-four red roses. She gave a great smile and tilted her head for a peck on the cheek; my peck missing her lips by less than an inch. And then I managed a light hug.

In the afternoon we took Simran to Hamleys, claiming to be the world's biggest toy store. A chauffeured Bentley was hired for the day. I feel more relaxed being driven in London than driving about.

I bought Simran a 2 ft. high Japanese doll, a Movado wristwatch, and a pair of skates. Rammi pitched in with a harmonica. And then Simran was taken to the Swiss Centre for high tea: cucumber sandwiches, pastries, hot chocolate and ice cream.

My birthday present to Rammi this year was a pair of gold-encased pearl earrings and a matching bracelet bought from Garrard on Regent Street. It would be a delight looking at the beauty of the familiar face, framed within these pearly earrings.

Looking into the store's mirror, she gave me a heart-stopping smile. "I would love to wear these most of the time," exclaimed an excited Rammi.

Late in the evening I took Rammi to dinner at the Ritz. Simran was left in the care of the lady housekeeper. Rammi was clad in a pink chiffon sari that clung to her model-like body and a thin blouse to match. She had kept her long flowing hair loose; this drawing appreciative looks from those around. Indeed, Bwana with the towering athletic figure and his beautiful companion made a dazzling couple.

The Ritz boasts of a dazzling dining room. And we had a table at a prime spot. A bottle of top Beaujolais priced at £70, was ordered. Rammi hardly drank. But being her birthday, she was persuaded to sip some of it. Between us we finished the bottle. After a fine meal of smoked salmon and New Zealand lamb, it was a slice of Black Forest cake (with the compliments of the management), the two servers singing "Happy Birthday." Thereafter, we had espresso with cognac.

It had been a fantastic evening, both of us full of cheer. Buoyed by alcohol, Rammi loosened up. Reminisced about her girlhood and the pranks she played in school. She omitted mention of any premarital love affair despite being prodded. Hard to believe such a pretty girl had none.

I spoke of my growing fascination for her, starting right from the moment I set eyes on her.

She allowed me to hold her hand. I escorted her out with an arm around her waist.

On reaching home, we lingered in the living room, put Frank Sinatra on the CD player; the night was still young for retiring to bed. I poured a Vintage port for myself and made her sip some. "I'm already tipsy," she mumbled.

For years I've been looking at her face; the dimpled cheeks, the bright eyes and the velvety skin. Yet what had struck me most was the thick lower lip slightly hung down. My greatest fantasy had been to hold that lip between mine.

It seemed the time had come to fulfill the years-old dream. I grasped her by the waist and took her lower lip between mine. In her turn, she clung to me, almost collapsed against my tall body. I roamed my tongue in her mouth. I was delirious and kept on the kiss as if I would suck the whole of her into me. It was the longest kiss of my life and the most exciting. She withdrew as if exhausted.

I slid my hand into her blouse and bra. The touch of the velvety firm mounds was electric. These breasts I had been seeing for over twelve years, always wondering what they would feel like. And I thought she did fail to notice the bulge in my trousers.

Rammi panicked. The atmosphere and the drink did loosen her control a bit but soon she recovered. She was in no mood for infidelity, even when she had been attracted to me. She pulled out my hand, disengaged herself from the hug, and rushed to her room, bolting it from inside.

Evidently her conscience had been pricked.

What had been Raminder's version of the kiss?

This day, the 15th of August, was my birthday.

Pity, Udai wasn't there; he has been called back to India on official duty. Udai was ever trying to make my birthday a memorable one. He gave me an expensive Gucci handbag before leaving for India. Frankly, I like people fussing over my birthday. And mine was no ordinary day—it's the country's Independence Day.

At thirty-two, the years were creeping up on me. The dreaded middle-age, I suppose, was still sometime away. Hope I can keep it at bay a little longer with exercise and diet control.

Sarabjeet happened to be the host on this birthday. He greeted me at breakfast with a bunch of twenty-four red roses (not thirty-two) and a beautiful birthday card. He was a dear. I knew he was in love with me, though he hadn't said so in so many words. I could easily figure out that love in his eyes.

Over the years he has given us company, heaped gifts on us, taken us on jaunts, entertained us, and has been a pillar of strength. He had come closer than a family member. Udai befriended him, Simran adored him. Recently he got her a brown pony, a round-bellied Shetland, named Lucy. The little mare was obedient to every pressure of Simran's legs. Simran's face would light up seeing Lucy, and the mare whinnies in response. Lucy would even come near if loose and nuzzle Simran for a piece of sugar. Simran in turn would feed her a few sugar cubes. The mare would then rub Simran in the ribs, as if asking her to take a ride.

Bwana gave me a pair of pearl earrings, two large pearls beautifully mounted in gold and a matching pearl bracelet. What a great gift! These will remind me of the gift-giver whenever I wear them—and I propose to wear them most of the time.

The day was topped with an exclusive dinner at the Ritz, with Bwana playing the perfect host.

To be frank, I've grown increasingly fond of him. There has never been a jarring moment, never an embarrassing situation, indeed never a boring encounter between us during all these years. To me he symbolized fun and gaiety, closeness and adulation.

Is this love?

I love Udai. But, I assume, you can love two men at the same time. I mean, love them in different ways. Actually I love both of them. That's the truth, whether people believe it or not.

This birthday evening turned out differently. For the first time sexual play erupted between the two of us.

Maybe I got a bit tipsy with those sips of wine, brandy, and port. I'm no good at holding alcohol.

And my condition may have encouraged him to stray from his customary reserve.

Standing close in the living room on return from the dinner, he took me in a sudden tight hug and kissed me long and hard. This caught me rather by surprise. I tried to wriggle out, avert my face. Maybe it was too mild a show of resistance on my part.

He continued with it. Kept on saying he loved me, loved me from the moment he saw me. And he did succeed in slipping a hand into my blouse and bra.

This was going too far. I had to put a stop to it. Hastily I pulled out his hand and hurried to my room, bolting it from inside.

It was past midnight. By now it must be sunrise in India. Udai should be up; he happened to be an early riser.

What's done is done, can't be undone. No regrets.

And my love and admiration for Sarabjeet was in no way diminished. After all, sexual intimacy is the one thing men ever want, and the best of them can experience a weak moment in the sort of situation he found himself in.

Yet I made up my mind on that occasion itself that there would be no repeat between us; I owed that to my marriage and Udai's loving trust.

5 A Genial Host

Sarabjeet was the best known host in the city. And much of his hospitality was at his residence itself.

Devi House was one of the few residences in Jaipur that boasted of central air-conditioning, backed-up by a 100 kilo-watt generator embedded in a corner of its grounds. This took care of the erratic electric supply. Yet you had to brave sweltering Jaipur summer heat, even a blistering dust storm, when you stirred out at midday. The city's water supply stood supplemented with a tubewell to cater for all those lawns and flowerpots. In fact, the front lawn was as large as a mini park.

Devi House was known for its hospitality. Bwana would give a dinner or a cocktail nearly once a week. The drinks and the food offered were of the highest quality.

Quite often Bwana got people together for dinner, lunch, or cocktail to fete a visiting friend. His circle of acquaintances spanned countries and continents. He could well be the leading host in the city, a city that attracted no few notable outsiders. Devi House was particularly entertaining for cocktail parties.

The main reception room with its white marble floor and two big chandeliers could hold around fifty guests. The square hall's principal decoration was a bronze statue of a horse that Bwana had ordered with Sehgal, a known Delhi sculptor. The statue was in proportion 1:4 and appeared to have been modelled on Bwana's favourite polo pony, Rani, the Argentinean mare. On the walls, were fixed a few polo mallets. And there were photographs of various polo teams and matches. A stuffed tiger head stood fixed on another wall and so also a pair of old family swords.

Later, when Bwana could play no more polo with his paralyzed legs, Raminder had once remarked, "Better put on a few paintings in place of polo photographs." He agreed and secured in time two paintings of Maqbool Fida Husain.

On one side of the reception room was a bar, rivalling a hotel bar. Various liquors arranged therein and a uniformed barman serving behind. There would be the well selected guest-list. High quality drinks were served liberally. Even glasses of drinks holding ice cubes were fitted with jackets so that guests didn't get their fingers wet. Tasty snacks would be in plenty; chicken tikka, fish fingers, and paneer pakoras. The drinks and the snacks were usually served by two of Bwana's servants, one tall one short, both wearing white trousers and white coats. In the absence of a hostess, Raminder was expected to keep an unobtrusive eye that everything went on smoothly.

In the end, only Udai and his wife, Dr. Adoor, and some selected friends would often stay on. They would forego a regular dinner—just have desert followed by coffee and cognac.

At the cocktail party, Udai and another polo-playing Cavalry officer, Karnail, generally regaled the listeners with jokes and sallies, at times bawdy. They would manage to collect a few pretty female listeners and amuse them with their witty talk. Udai enjoyed narrating an incident where a new entrant to the regiment, a burly second lieutenant was at a polo practice session. His kit had been delayed in transit. A colleague had lent him his old pair of riding breeches. With quite a few of us watching including the colonel's wife, his borrowed breeches snapped at the hips when he flung his leg over the horse for mounting. As luck would have it, he wasn't supporting underwear. In embarrassment the poor fellow rode straight to the barracks and got into his own trousers. Raminder, passing by, was apt to frown at this sort of joke. Even Bwana looked more for cordiality than horseplay in his parties.

He would often ask a guest to have his or her drink refilled. Yet he was in no mood to overlook drunken behaviour. He himself was a temperate drinker, mainly content with a glass or two of wine.

His guests found it rather easy to locate him, being six feet one, in a crowded cocktail party.

Bwana's two largest parties marked Diwali, a goodbye to the long hot summer, and Holi, signaling the end of the short, invigorating winter of Jaipur. These two parties stood as highlights of Bwana's hospitality. People always felt nice to be included in the guest-list.

Devi House would be tastefully lighted for Diwali with hundreds of diyas and candles; Bwana didn't fancy electric bulbs. And the design of the house with its several long terraces lent itself to a brilliant sight with the Diwali lighting.

The evening function would start with fireworks. Guests were asked to bring their children along as the crackers were of special interest to youngsters. Bigger boys were even encouraged to operate some of these fireworks. Bwana would spend several thousand rupees on this aspect of entertainment. Meantime, a liquor bar would be set-up at the side of the front lawn and another one was there in the house itself. On offer would be choice whiskies, such as Black Label whisky, single malts, and fine French wines. Over a hundred guests milled around either in the lawn or in the hall-like reception area and adjoining rooms. People would come out to see fireworks, hear the deafening noise, put their hands on their ears and retreat inside. Around ten, a lavish buffet meal would be there with tables seating six each. And the caterers would serve hot tandoori chicken and other roasted items, besides the main meal. They would also pour red or white wines into glasses.

Bwana mostly stationed himself at the entrance receiving visitors as they came in and would be there to see them off as they left. He took care to welcome guests quickly so as not to form a longish queue of people waiting to be welcomed.

Yet he always had nice words for his guests, especially ladies. He would put in words of praise for a lady's outfit, her ornaments, or general appearance. To many winsome women guests, he would address them as Sundari or Sweetie. Bwana was particularly popular with the ladies. He never used any lewd words or physical advances. Any intimate talk was reserved for Raminder and that, too, in private.

Diwali evening at Devi House with its mild Jaipur weather had become a known feature of the city's elite. It was not the place for longish card sessions associated with Diwali. Bwana didn't fancy card game, particularly those with high stakes.

Holi celebration could turn fairly boisterous, even at times getting rowdy. An innovation started by Bwana was to send a couple of open trucks to collect selected friends and their families. This way, persons in his close circle could come without the risk of their cars being damaged en route by Holi hooligans.

The Holi revelers dressed in their white clothes would get drenched with coloured water from syringes and balloons. Pretty women were particularly targets of such fun. Some men who seemed to be backing out were bodily lifted and ducked into tubs of coloured water. A soft drink, mostly *shardai*, was served laced with *bhang*. And there was beer and gin for those who preferred alcohol.

The people would start gathering on a lawn by 11:00 a.m. While some will go back, most others stayed on for lunch, a veritable feast of vegetarian food served to some 200 people in the open itself. To Bwana's friends and acquaintances, the Holi merrymaking at his place was something to wait for and remember.

After the polo accident that left Bwana without the use of his legs, he still continued to be a genial host.

Inside his house, Bwana could move with the help of a walker or crutches. But when he had to stand for a longer period there was no escape from the use of wheelchair, especially in a largish party where he needed mobility to talk with many of his guests. Of course, when he had to attend function at other people's houses or hotels, it had to be the wheelchair. Ordinarily, he would avoid going to a place where stairs had to be climbed. At best he could manage three to four steps with the help of a strong railing. With the upper body becoming more powerful with exercise and swimming, managing a wheelchair came easy to him.

At one time short people had the awkwardness to look up to the tall Bwana for talking. Now with him in the wheelchair they were looking down to him. In turn Bwana learnt to make the necessary adjustment.

In the beginning Bwana did feel awkward and funny when unable to stand on his legs. But over the years he got reconciled to his handicap. He would even joke about it.

Sarabjeet was slowly sliding into the altered daily routine. Instead of an hour's morning ride, it meant a longish yoga routine under the guidance of a known yoga teacher. Thereafter it was an hour of physiotherapy. The trained physiotherapist not only did a competent job, he regaled Bwana all the time with witty talk and funny stories. A good deal of time was spent on exercises of the back. To his surprise, these were mostly the exercises of legs and feet; he never imagined the legs and feet were so crucially connected to the back. The yoga teacher and physiotherapist would mostly concentrate attention on his feet—pressing them, putting pressure on various nerves, and doing vigorous rubbing. The yoga teacher would explain that various nerves in the back reach down to the feet. And then he had all those exercises that strengthened the neck; twisting the neck, rotating shoulders, etc. The breathing and meditation part of yoga was supposed to calm down his restive mind.

The afternoon polo or tennis stood replaced by swimming in the house pool. He had it enclosed as well as heated for winter. Hours of swimming had strengthened muscles of his arms and chest. In fact, he had grown very strong in the upper part of his body.

Bwana was still keeping up with his lavish entertaining. It could come to dozens of invitees at cocktail or select dinner parties once a week. And he rarely ate alone; there was some invitee or houseguest to join in, let alone the twin daughters.

However, the accustomed jollity of gatherings at his place had yet to resurface. A subtle shift was also evident in the guest-list itself. Polo players and their wives began to figure less prominently. He missed the polo gang; hard-drinking men with their joviality and ribald jokes; wives daringly clad, drinking well, probably horny in bed, who could be mocking among themselves about male sexual demands as impatient but short in staying power. At times the polo gang would break into a song with one of them sitting at the Steinway piano. They would persuade women to dance with them, both Udai and Bwana were graceful dancers, and so was Raminder.

Bwana didn't smoke. At the most it was a cigar or cheroot after a very satisfying dinner. Yet there were quite a few of his polo friends, Udai included, who were avid smokers. The main reception room boasted of an alcove, shorn of carpets and rugs. Those who had to smoke would move to the alcove. Interestingly, there was a complete absence of ashtrays in the reception area.

At Bwana's parties you now saw more of top-rung officials, businessmen, politicians, and medical specialists; a relatively sober, self-opinionated, self-conscious, less lively lot. The men mostly talked politics with their innate tendency to explain what they knew best.

The women seated in groups gossiped about clothes, servant problems, and children troubles. When pushed for an alcoholic drink, the usual ladylike response, "But a small one, please." The genial host in turn would get them a regular measure. Even returns in time for a refill.

Bwana was keen to show to his friends and others that he functioned more or less as before. Yet in his heart he knew fully well that his life had undergone a terrible change with the loss of his legs.

6 Coping with Udai's Demise

"Rammi, you visit Devi House so rarely these days," complained Bwana.

There was no response from Rammi.

"We used to see each other almost every evening at my place or at yours. Udai's death has brought a big void in your life, and even in mine. Yet we have to live our lives."

Raminder—Rammi to Udai and close friends—wasn't her former picture of liveliness. She dressed demurely, hardly used any make-up. And she hadn't resumed her morning ride at the Cavalry grounds or at Bwana's farm. Instead, she took a dozen lessons from a known yoga teacher. Her morning routine now included around one hour of yoga, both for keeping a perfect figure and some peace of mind. This daily routine did help her in maintaining a trim figure full of vitality right into her late years.

Yet, her former cheerfulness never returned. Indeed, her heart ached with the absence of Udai whom she had loved dearly, and he was her main support in life. She would recall her happy years with Udai and cry silently into the night. However, she had to maintain a brave front for the sake of Simran who also loomed forlorn with her missing father.

Meantime, Raminder had to shift from the roomy, well-kept bungalow in the Cantonment to Udai's ancestral house in the walled city where his widowed mother Bhago stayed.

In fact, Bhago had come to live in the army bungalow when Simran was born. Her idea was to help the mother and the child.

Bhago in her seventies had developed a stoop; thin and tall, she must have had a presentable figure in her youth. However, she stuck to her strict code of a wife's total fidelity to her husband.

She would have stayed longer at the army bungalow but the old woman was hearing gossip of an affair between Raminder and Bwana. This suspicion got firmed up with Bwana's frequent visits to Udai's place. The whole thing disturbed her greatly. However, instead of taking the matter with her son Udai or even directly with her daughter-in-law she thought it prudent to go back and live in the family's city haveli.

Now that Raminder had to live in the haveli itself, Bhago in time went back to the old thikana house, the family's original place in the village near Jodhpur. The old woman had no stomach to live with her daughter-in-law, more so when Bwana's visits could become more frequent.

It was a bit of disappointment to Raminder that Udai's two younger brothers did not assist her in any manner. Indeed, they ultimately managed that she got no portion of the ancestral property that would have been Udai's share. Possibly, their minds poisoned by rumours of Raminder's relationship with Bwana.

Notwithstanding considerable assistance by Bwana, the old haveli had yet to shape into anything comfortable. The run-down dwelling called for extensive renovations in flooring, new electric fittings, modern plumbing, comfortable bathroom, and an acceptable kitchen. The move heralded a daunting change from the open green spaces of the cantonment to crowded, noisy city lanes. And, instead of a team of alert and efficient orderlies and attendants, she had the sole services of one slovenly maid, and a driver lent by Bwana for the family's Maruti 800.

At the cantonment bungalow whenever there was a fuse burnt or a tap leaked it just needed telling the orderly. Workers would come and set the thing right the same day. Now for any little thing she had to chase workers, and when they came, they asked for money that looked like daylight robbery. Male plumbers, carpenters and electricians weren't easy for a woman to tackle, she found. Of course, in case of a real emergency she could always ring up Bwana's office.

Lucky, she got an insurance claim of rupees ten lakh. Only a year before, the policy had been taken.

"Udai, insure yourself against a polo accident," Bwana had said one evening, "A foreign company with a branch in India is now extending such cover. I have one already."

"What's the point? The army looks after us when we sustain injuries."

"It's a small annual premium that accords you full cover."

Rammi, handing out snacks, joined in, "Bwana's idea of insurance seems sound. You play so much polo, and I'd say you play dangerously."

While Udai was still mocking at the idea, sipping his Scotch, Bwana mentioned, "I'd be sending the insurance agent tomorrow. Rammi, you see Udai signs the form."

"I will. And sending premiums will be my responsibility."

Rammi was struck with another tragedy. Her father suffered a severe heart attack early one morning and died before medical help could arrive. After being with her son for a few months at Ludhiana, the General's widow came to stay with Raminder.

Gurpal Kaur was a stout, well-built woman of fifty-five who dressed in nicely tailored salwar-kameez suits and took regular walks for exercise. She could well last another twenty-five years. The only weakness was her set of false teeth and quite a few facial freckles. Simran was amused no end when Gurpal Kaur took off her teeth at night, placing them in a bowl having a cleansing agent. The mother seemed to have settled down at Jaipur on a long haul.

Gurpal Kaur had never taken kindly to Raminder's known familiarity with Sarabjeet. With Udai gone, she grew increasingly critical of this liaison. She frowned on more than a weekly visit from Bwana, and tolerated that only because he was ever extending them assistance through his money and contacts. Yet Bwana remained invariably polite and considerate to the doughty Sikh matron.

Simran, on the contrary, was moving closer to Sarabjeet, ever her favourite "uncle". Maybe she found in him a substitute for her missing father. Simran frequented Devi House, swam regularly in the pool, went on drives with Bwana in his BMW Boxter with the hood off, and usually returned home loaded with gifts. Bwana's mansion anyway was a welcome change from their old, dreary haveli.

"Why you've to go almost every day from school to Devi House?" her grandma was apt to ask with a knitted brow as she saw Simran getting dropped late in the evening, "When would you do your homework?"

"I finish homework at uncle's place. His secretary helps me with it."

"We'd help you here. Girls must come home directly after school. You could learn some cooking, too."

"Don't worry Nanni Ji. I'll learn cooking in good time if I have to."

During all these altercations Rammi would remain a mere bemused spectator.

Gurpal Kaur knew she could do jolly little to rein in the girl—rather a headstrong youngster with a mind of her own.

"You and Simran need a holiday badly, a break," Sarabjeet told Rammi one muggy evening in August, "Why don't you go for some days to my villa in Shimla?"

"That would be fun," Simran exclaimed. She had happy memories of Shimla jaunts with him. Rammi appeared noncommittal.

"If my presence would prove a deterrent you can be on your own. Balwindar would drive you there, be with you, and bring you back."

"No, it's not that," said Rammi, finding hard to hide a blush.

"Then what's the hitch? Better go now as I will be selling the villa. I'm in no physical condition to walk in the hills."

"Will let you know in a day or two," as she brushed away a strand of hair from her forehead.

Eventually, the trip didn't materialize. To Gurpal Kaur, it would be a holiday too soon after Udai's demise, let alone smacking of undue proximity to Bwana.

Apparently the mother wasn't fully conversant with Bwana's favours to the family, and the ways in which Rammi had been reciprocating.

On Sarabjeet's side, it'd be the live-in twin daughter Kranti who rates Rammi a rival to her standing with Bwana and a threat to the family fortune. Her worst fear was of her father marrying the widow. Mother and daughter coming to live in the house—in fact, taking it over—was a prospect she simply dreaded.

Kranti, however, had to keep her hostility low key. Bwana wasn't the one to brook open defiance to his wishes.

Part-II

Part-II

7 Birth of Twins

Sarabjeet was the eldest born to the head of Tikam thikana, a petty jagir some fifty miles from Jaipur. Besides the ancestral fort-like hilltop mansion in Tikam, the family owned a sprawling haveli in the walled Jaipur city.

From a promising start in school, Sarabjeet was sent to Mayo College, Ajmer. In this prestigious college, originally meant for sons of chieftains, Sarabjeet stayed undistinguished in studies. Yet he was a star horseman, the institution's best tennis player and captain of the college basketball team.

By the time he was seventeen, he had shot to a height of six feet one. Trim, muscular, broad shouldered, with a lady-killer nose and piercing brown eyes, he cut a fine figure. With his short clipped moustache on a firm jaw line and neatly-parted hair, his classmates likened him to Clarke Gable.

Sarabjeet was tipped to go for higher studies in UK. At this juncture the father died in a hotel room in Pune under mysterious circumstances. The local police eventually closed the case as one of suicide from an overdose of heroin. The family didn't seek closer investigation or greater publicity; a call-girl was known to be with him that night.

At one time Sarabjeet entertained a strong desire to trace out the woman in question to ascertain the exact circumstances of his father's death. But then he feared that the woman might start blackmailing him by threatening to spill the beans to the press. Such publicity could hurt his rising social image and burgeoning business.

By the time of his father's death, family finances had become precarious. Income from landholdings had shrunk. And there was the father's living style—losing money at races and expensive whoring.

Sarabjeet's contacts with his father were minimal. During his childhood he saw very little of him. All he could remember was a handsome tall man often out hunting or travelling to other places. At the age of seven he had been moved with Mother to the Jaipur haveli for his schooling. Father mainly lived at the tikhana and so also Sarabjeet's younger brother. That way a special bond had developed between Sarabjeet and his mother. She was a slim, gaunt woman who had a rather unhappy marriage to a philandering husband.

The family finances had been worsening during his father's lifetime. Happily, his mother had been able to retain the ancestral accumulation of jewellery, gold mohurs, and heavy silverware.

Sarabjeet left the day-to-day management of the thikana to his younger brother Prem Singh who stayed on at Tikam. Himself, he chose to live in Jaipur, looking after what little property was left there, while he hoped to revive the family fortune through some business venture.

His mother Kamla had started ailing from an undiagnosed illness, possibly a stomach cancer. She was having painful cramps in her stomach and heaviness in the head.

"Sarbo, you're a real good son," she said, as he busied nursing her.

"We'll get you the best medical aid."

"That would be wasting money and effort. I know I'm dying. My dearest wish, if you ask me, is to see you married in my lifetime."

"Don't talk of death. There could be some cure for you. I am in contact with two of the best doctors in Swai Mansingh Hospital. They are counselling me to move you to the hospital itself."

"Sarbo, it is all futile. There is no hope for me. I would like to die in my own bed than be rushed around in hospital."

As a compromise, Sarabjeet got her a qualified nurse and visits by two eminent doctors. Despite all types of medication, her condition was worsening day by day. It seemed that she might not have more than a few months to live.

Willy-nilly, to comfort the terminally ill mother, he accepted marriage to a jagirdar's daughter from his mother's side, though he had no inclination to marry at this unsettled stage of his life. He had only seen her once for a few fleeting moments.

Sarabjeet was 21 and his bride 17. The marriage took place with the customary Rajput pomp and show, knocking another hole in the family finances.

Durga Devi, a high-school pass, was pretty as a picture; a marble-smooth body and a shining pair of eyes looming large on her narrow face. She was somewhat on the frail side. Durga Devi charmed everyone with her looks and modest behaviour. Sarabjeet grew very fond of her; indeed, fell in love with her.

Within months of the marriage his mother died. Her only consolation: Durga was pregnant.

Tests indicated that Durga was bearing twins. Discussing twins, Bwana's doctor friend, Sodhi was somewhat surprised at the development. "Normally, twins are a feature of strongly built mothers, the nature's precaution to provide maximum nutrition to the foetus in the womb. Twins for a mother as delicate as Durga are a rarity. The twins would be putting much pressure on her bodily resources."

Doctors prescribed a stricter regime of care and frequent pre-natal check-ups.

Sarabjeet persuaded Paro, the younger sister of his mother, to come and stay with them. Paro, forty, was a childless widow, a small shriveled woman who rarely smiled. Her housekeeping help was deemed essential in view of Durga's advanced pregnancy. Paro was a willing worker. She helped to run the household. Paro did supervise the physical needs of the twins but was not happy to live in Jaipur. She longed for her own village life. And when the twins began attending kindergarten, in an English medium school, she was at a loss to help them, being almost illiterate.

There was the double load and Durga's delicate health, coupled with the complication of incipient diabetes. The delivery would necessarily be in a hospital.

Durga's family had a history of twins. She herself came with a twin brother.

Two underweight twins, both girls, arrived within 9 minutes of each other. To Rajputs, with their marked preference for boys, it was a bit dismaying that a baby girl surfaced. And, lo, after a nine-minute wait, another baby girl appeared.

The doctors were unable to save the frail, diabetic mother, more so with the heavy bleeding of the uterus.

Sarabjeet was desolate. His loving wife was dead in her youth, and he was landed with the care of twin baby girls in delicate health. The twins, weighing a fraction less than six pounds each, had to be kept in the ICU for a fortnight and another ten days in the hospital.

He was devastated with the loss of Durga. She was such a loveable being; cheerful, soft-spoken, smiling even when in pain, with chiselled features and a silken-smooth body. He was deeply in love with her, his first love.

On bringing the twins home, two wet nurses were arranged; two buxom rural mothers from the thikana. The baby girls took away a lot of his time and attention at a juncture when he was frenetically on the lookout for an opening in business.

Once, his curiosity was tickled as to how human milk tasted. With the intervention of Paro he did manage to have a spoonful squeezed from one of the nannies. To his surprise, he didn't find it tasty while the little girls sucked merrily. He wondered why infants loved it so.

The twins were very beautiful to look at. Both the girls had learnt to smile. Sarabjeet took much time looking at them and fondling them—two dainty creatures with bright open eyes and soft rosy cheeks.

Twins invariably excite interest. This is the reaction not only of relatives and neighbours but also even of strangers. People can't help comparing twins. You hear talk of the Ramayana's Luv and Kush. One uncle went on to mention the Roman twins, Romulus and Remus (with one killing the other).

Genetic tests revealed that the two baby girls were DZ (fraternal) twins, resulting from two separately released ova, and not MZ (identical) twins from an early division of a single egg.

Fraternal twins are, in their genetic make-up, like any two siblings; they can even be of different sexes. Where they differ from normal siblings is the fact of sharing the womb together. The first twin, they say, enjoys certain advantages in physical terms. The pre-natal mortality rate is much higher for the second-born twin, more so if the second delivery is delayed beyond twenty minutes. Luckily, Kranti (meaning "revolution") emerged within nine minutes of Shanti (meaning "peace"), though she did give the attending doctors a few anxious moments.

Sarabjeet was amused, actually amazed, as he noticed the twins grown up. The two babies seemed to take delight in looking at each other, smile at each other, babbling with each other, and playing with each other. If one cried, the other cried. If one chortled, the other chortled. He found that the world of twins till they are three or four mainly centered on each other as if the other was more interesting than anything else. It was only when they were around five that the girls started developing some separate interests.

"The most crucial point in the upbringing of twins is to develop their separate identity from the very start," said Dr Sodhi, Sarabjeet's psychiatrist friend, while sharing a drink with him. "You may be aware of this imperative but its implementation would call for continued vigilance on your part."

"That way we have already erred in giving them similar-sounding names."

"What's done is done. And the names are nice. Luckily, the two girls don't look alike. The elder one is fairer with a strikingly beautiful face. The younger one, by contrast is dusky and the facial features less sharp than her sister. Henceforth, the girls must sleep in separate beds, preferably in separate rooms. Better keep two nannies. The twins should wear different dresses. Have different hairstyles. Put them in different schools, at least in different sections if still in the same school. Even their birthday can be celebrated in two separate functions, say one for the elder at noon and the other in the evening. Presents need not be identical."

"All this will appear a little odd. Yet I see no difficulty in providing them with separate nannies, clothing them differently, and giving them different hairstyles."

"The main objective," Sodhi explained, "is to think consistently of the twins as two individuals with their own talents, likes, dislikes, and personalities."

"It's my deep wish that the two girls develop their individuality. And that's the minimum I owe to my dear departed wife."

Little did Sarabjeet foresee that the twins would acquire such contrasting personalities, he would be hard put to help them get along.

Of course, he deemed himself lucky in one respect. He got two kids at one go.

8 Twins Grow Up

The twins were now twelve.

Four years back the family moved out of the sprawling ancestral haveli in the walled city to a new mansion set in sylvan surroundings. Of course, as walled cities go, Jaipur is possibly the best planned. Built some 250 years back, it boasts of straight roads, some as wide as 120 feet. Houses and shops facing the main roads are all plastered pink. And the walled city retains its eminence as a trade and business hub.

At this juncture, Paro indicated that her knees were giving a lot of trouble. She would prefer to go back and rest at her place. She also mentioned that she won't be able to manage in a house with modern plumbing and other advanced gadgets. Sarabjeet had no option but to relieve her. Paro was given a sum of ₹. 5000 and an expensive suit of clothes despite her protestation to the contrary. And he arranged her visit back in one of his cars. Paro's presence had proved a boon while the twins were small.

Bwana felt the need to have a professional live-in housekeeper to look after the house and the girls.

The twins were overjoyed at the change from a crowded locality and old-fashioned house to open spaces, greenery, lawns, swimming pool, and modern plumbing. Both girls had a suite each, with one sunlit room for study and play, the other as bedroom with an adjoining tub-fitted bathroom.

The housekeeper, a spinster of forty-five, had her room adjoining the girls section. Nirmala was a plump heavy-breasted woman with a fair complexion, sporting a biggish gold nose-pin. You could see hair growing on her upper lip. She said that she hailed from Kashmir. She was seen taking much care about her grooming and clothes, considering herself as still attractive to men.

Her job was to sort out the clothes of the twins and other articles of use. And she helped them in bathing, playing, and study. With Sarabjeet required to visit places outside Jaipur, Nirmala was the one entrusted with the care of the girls. She was also doing her bit to work out their pre-puberty problems.

The two girls would often question their dad about the mother, the one who had died at their birth. Bwana would bring out an album and show them the photographs of their mother at the age of five, at the age of nine, and several pictures of the marriage ceremony. He would tell them how beautiful and charming their mother was!

Bwana had stored some of the belongings of his dead wife in a wooden box. There were the clothes which she had worn at the marriage ceremonies, all silk with gold work. There was a hand-held looking glass which Durga Devi used to have and so also a few of her ornaments, the one Bwana didn't give away. There was a diamond wedding ring, a pearl necklace and half a dozen gold bangles. It also included a pair of sandals decorated with silver stripes. And then there was an enlarged photograph of Durga Devi, a studio photograph taken some days after marriage. Another one was of Sarabjeet and Durga Devi together. At the wish of the twins, a photograph of their mother was hung in each of their rooms.

The box also contained some baby clothes and a few knitted socks, collected by Durga Devi for the coming twins. More elaborate clothes were to wait till the sex of the babies was known.

Shanti studied in the noted Maharani Gayatri Devi All-Girls School, Kranti in the premier St. Xavier School, a co-educational institute. Both were in grade VII.

Shanti was average in studies. She could easily do better if she concentrated. But sustained attention eluded her; her mind tended to wander off whenever she was attending to anything serious.

Shanti had a singing voice, and was taking regular piano lessons. She was fond of dressing well. Her room was kept tidy; books and clothes nicely arranged, with an array of Japanese dolls. She already behaved like a little lady.

Kranti was top in studies. Non-serious in class, she read a lot at home, mostly late at night in bed. Reading all those Enid Blyton novels gave her a better hold on the English language than many of her classmates.

Her rooms mostly lay littered with things thrown about, at times giving the appearance of a battlefield. She did well in sports, such as short-distance running, badminton, and basketball, let alone being good at riding.

On the swing positioned near the pool she would kick and soar high, the ropes getting taut, the frame shake as she reached the horizontal stage. Still, she would kick higher, her feet up in the sky.

Careless of her appearance, Kranti was turning out a virtual tomboy. She once hit an annoying bulky classmate hard on his head with her badminton racquet. Broke the racquet; damage to the targeted skull remained unreported.

At home Shanti behaved rather responsibly, more possessively, as if enjoying the prerogative of the first-born. And she did manage to secure greater fatherly attention.

Kranti acted more secretive, more rebellious, the typical later-born behaviour, though she was late by no more than nine minutes. And she could be quite rude to Shanti when the latter tried to show off or behave bossy. Shanti knew very well that if it came down to fisticuffs, she would be at the receiving end.

And the occasion did actually arise once. Kranti hadn't appeared at Sunday breakfast despite the servant sent to call her.

"I'll go get her," said Shanti, acting as virtual hostess at the table.

She found Kranti in bed reading a Mills and Boon novel.

"You lazy bones, come for breakfast quickly."

"I'm in the midst of a captivating love scene. Will come later, or better send my breakfast here."

"Breakfast can't come here. Get up," and she gave a sharp pull to Kranti's leg sticking out of the duvet.

Kranti threw the paperback at the elder twin, and it scraped her stomach. Shanti picked up the book and flung it back at Kranti. As luck would have it the book's hard spine hit Kranti right on the nose. In fury she jumped out of the bed and landed a fist blow on Shanti. Her fist missed the nose, but hit Shanti on the temple. The blow was so hard Shanti stood stunned. Tears rolled down her cheeks.

"I'm reporting this to Dad," and she fled from the room.

Bwana listened patiently to Shanti. He comforted her with a hug. "I'll talk to Kranti. Ask her to behave, even apologize." He was the father as well as the mother of the twins, and didn't want to do anything that could hurt one of the two.

He beckoned the servant to take the breakfast tray to Kranti's room, the tray containing a French toast, slices of pear, a glass of chocolate milk, and five water-soaked almonds.

Yet the twins weren't in a perpetual state of competition or conflict. They invariably supported each other against outside boys or girls. Kranti was particularly protective of Shanti whom she deemed soft and mild. The two stayed long hours together, playing, swimming, or running about in the house and the farm. And they were liberal in lending each other books, toys, even items of wear.

It is made out that sharing the same womb; competing for the restricted space and nutrition can create some striking dissimilarities among twins. Quite a few of the twin differences are traceable to the early pre-natal stages: unequal nutrition, unequal blood supply.

"Twins tend to have lower IQ than singletons," said Dr. Sodhi, "because twins in the womb have to share the limited supply of nutrients. And so they would need extra inputs in education and food to come at par with singletons."

"Everything would be done to make up for this deficiency, if there's any," Sarabjeet assured his doctor friend.

At twelve, the two girls couldn't be more dissimilar. Dr Sodhi's advice of giving the twins their own individuality has been carried out quite well—some would say, too well.

9 Bwana's Lavish Lifestyle

While the twins were growing up, Sarabjeet was swept up by an amazing flood tide of financial fortune.

He now lived in a custom-built mansion adjacent to the Statue Circle, an elite city landmark. Earlier, the place was a rundown guest house with an extensive area of shrubs and trees. Bwana bought the place, demolished the guest house, and cleared the surrounding grounds. Sited amidst a large swath of greenery, the building had the open spaces of the Palace grounds in front. The polo ground and the golf course were just across. In the memory of his deceased wife Durga Devi, the house was named "Devi House".

It was a 2-storey palatial stone building that had a lush lawn in front, a swimming pool at the side. There was a guest wing and a clay tennis court. The chandeliered reception room could take some fifty, and the heavy rose wood dining table sat twenty. Bwana was particularly proud of the fifty-year-old table that he had bought from the Maharaja of Jodhpur.

His own living quarters were on the first floor consisting of a sitting room, a bedroom, a side room, and a bathroom. Right across was another set of rooms of the same type but smaller and not so lavishly furnished. The twins lived at the ground floor along with the house-keeper.

Sarabjeet's hobby was collecting exotic watches of all types. You saw two large glass shelves full of fancy wristwatches, pocket watches, and bedside watches. The whole collection numbering over a hundred must be worth a fortune.

The bar, a favoured haunt among friends, matched a five-star hotel bar in dimensions, fixtures, and variety of drinks. Bwana was sparing in alcohol intake; normally, he took no more than a glass of classy wine or a small measure of dry sherry to keep company. A few of his companions, and that included Udai, drank heavily, mostly beer at noontime and Scotch at sundown.

And you often saw sprawled on the bar floor a pair of white poodles, named "Raja" and Rani", as if the animals fancied the smell of liquor. Tipsy guests had to be wary lest they stepped on an outstretched paw. Luckily, there were no long tails to be trampled upon, the dogs having merely a little bunch of it.

Bwana had managed to get this young pair through a friend in Singapore. The bitch was neutered. A friend had once joked that naming the dogs Raja and Rani could be a bit quirky in the land where they had actual rajas and ranis.

Bwana had grown very fond of the pair. They preferred to sleep near his bed at night. The poodle was deemed one of the most intelligent of dogs. The only problem was that the poodles had to be taken to a hair dressing saloon every two months for haircut; they don't shed hair like other dogs. Bwana used to say that whenever these dogs die, they would be replaced only by poodles.

Besides utility vehicles, three luxury cars were ranged in the garage section: a black Mercedes 220, a BMW3 convertible, and a silvery Volvo van. For bringing supplies and other errands, the staff used a small utility truck.

Six polo ponies and a brace of riding mounts were stabled at a farm five miles off on Ajmer Road. A self-contained cottage was built for the master of the horses. Bwana would keep a look out in the country and even abroad for good polo ponies and riding mounts. Horses fascinated him greatly; their looks, their intelligence, their spirit. Indeed, he was of the view that the horse was the most beautiful of the domesticated animals.

The 18-acre farm, with its own riding track and polo practice area, a three-par golf hole, a putting green, and an Olympic-size pool was backed by a Spanish-style villa. Fed by tubewells, a tiny rivulet ran through the campus. The farmhouse and its surroundings formed a frequent venue of Bwana's daytime entertaining in the winter, taking advantage of the Jaipur's mild weather at that time.

The farm also provided the city establishment with its daily requirements of milk, eggs, chicken, seasonal vegetables and fruits.

How did Sarabjeet come into the sort of money that enabled him to live in near regal style?

It all began with his selling off a sizeable part of the family's landholdings, land that was yielding poor income. To it was added the family's gold mohurs and some bank loans. The collected money enabled him to acquire fifty acres of farmland just outside the Jaipur municipal limits. Sarabjeet had the uncanny feel that the city would expand fast on that particular side.

As anticipated, the demand for land there shot up soon for office buildings, hotels, industrial units and warehouses, even luxury flats. Sarabjeet made a killing by selling off the acquired area in bits at fancy prices. It appears that luck is a form of talent—and this Sarabjeet seem to display in ample measure.

There was some opposition from the panchayat bosses and a few neighbourhood farmers. They were handsomely bribed to keep quiet.

Sarabjeet was lucky to have as assistant an incomparable troubleshooter, who was unmatched in tackling hurdles in land deals whether from private parties or from government quarters. And Rajpal had sufficient funds at his disposal to bribe his way through and silence opposition.

Clearly buying agriculture land or government land bristled with complications and difficulty. Sarabjeet had to keep in good humour the political bosses of the area as well as to cultivate the connected bureaucracy. Here, his genial personality, excellent contacts, and an ability to respond quickly to various bottlenecks gave him an edge in working out the project.

Buoyed by the success of the Jaipur venture and flush with funds, Sarabjeet bought about seventy acres of farmland in Gurgaon. A Mayo College classmate living in the vicinity proved a valuable contact and help. And this land soon turned into a gold mine, being parceled out at high prices to upscale housing estates, multi-storey flats, farm houses, high business blocks, and for part of a prized golf course. It is said that the sort of fast development that Gurgaon saw has not been matched anywhere in the world.

He was giving proof of an uncanny ability to anticipate correctly which area would be set for heady development. And he had honed the techniques of buying land quick and cheap—land that could be sold later to developers at hefty profit.

Sarabjeet shied from entering into the business of land development itself. This would entail a heavy charge on his time, attention and capital.

He really wanted to live a life of leisure that would include much riding, polo, and social mixing. His aim was to do half a dozen big deals in the coming decade or two, and then live luxuriously on the proceeds.

And he did make tons of money out of successful land deals at Dehradun, Haridwar and Faridabad. Yet his biggest coup was a major land acquisition venture near Pune.

He would visit Pune frequently for betting at horse races. It gave him some valuable contacts in the army and the horsing fraternity. One such contact assisted him in buying a vast chunk of land on the Pune–Bangalore highway. And rapid industrial development on that stretch was proving a windfall for him.

Of course, his land ventures were not without a failure or two. He had bought land outside NOIDA's town limits and was looking forward to its gainful disposal. But the U.P. government stepped in and acquired the land he had purchased. The compensation he got was very low. Sarabjeet had learnt to accept such a setback with equanimity. After all, he was a betting man.

By the time Sarabjeet was forty he had enough money to live a rich man's life. He still used his extraordinary flair to acquire land going cheap for selling it at the appropriate juncture to users and developers. His cash accumulation reached a point, where he became more interested in investing money in share market, mutual funds, and other long-term financial investments yielding high revenues. A part of his office set-up was now devoted entirely to investment planning. Even if Sarabjeet did not do any more land deals, the income generated from market investments was more than enough for his lavish lifestyle, let alone money given for various charities. Here, a special emphasis was on his schemes of girls' education, girls' hostels, and work-training for poor girls.

Working to earn money was no longer a priority with him.

The ancestral haveli with all its rooms, alcoves, and verandahs had been turned into an office for his general manager, PR officer, and legal-cum-accounting staff. Sarabjeet hardly went there; he operated from his home, assisted by a secretary and telephone clerk.

He was usually in his spacious library-cum-office from 10 a.m. up to lunch time, with a coffee break around 11:30. Bwana had grown fond of good coffee. He disdained instant coffee. An Italian coffee machine was installed and high quality Colombian roasted beans were used. He used to say that espresso was a special gift of Italy.

The office has a room with two large French windows opening on the front lawn. If you were so inclined, you could step out of an open window on to the lawn itself. Two walls lay ranged with books, mostly leather-bound novels including Dickens, Thackeray, Scott, Hardy, Jane Austen—a good many collected by his father. And sundry books on biography, travel, and politics were there and so also a row of *Britannica* encyclopedias, *Webster's* dictionaries, and *Who's Who*.

Bwana was no reader of books. Yet he liked to be surrounded by books. His real interest lay in newspapers and magazines. You saw a plethora of these spread out. Indeed, most of his conversational and business information was picked up from these publications, both Indian and foreign. *The Wall Street Journal*, London *Economist*, and *Newsweek* figured prominently in the foreign list.

The most striking feature of the room was his writing table. Sarabjeet had got the teak wood table built from his own specifications. He frowned on side drawers that could hamper the movement of his long legs. All in all it was a polished low table free of side drawers, the feet to be rested on a footrest. Bwana, generally, saw to it the table top remained free, uncluttered. Coasters had to be used for a cup of tea or coffee.

He could easily have a separate office room. Yet he preferred to sit in a section of the large library, as if his work was intellectual, not mundane money-making.

The actual work involved more phone calls than paperwork. An hour or so went in reviewing business matters with staff members. Occasionally, it might include visiting a top politician or a senior government official. Or, it could be a short business trip in the country. For an overnight halt he preferred to carry his own feather pillow. Most hotel pillows were no good, he would say. Bwana maintained excellent contacts with ministers and other bigwigs. He particularly cultivated top bureaucrats—inviting them to parties and entertainment at his place, giving gifts on suitable occasions, especially gifts that pleased their wives.

As to politics, he had leaning towards Congress. Yet he maintained cordial relations with the Jaipur royalty (that often stood opposition to Congress). He had also contacts with prominent BJP leaders and labour bosses.

At Pune he kept a field office. A hired security firm guarded his residence, farm, and various tracts of lands still not disposed off.

Sarabjeet's strongest point: he made no enemies, because he never spoke ill of anybody and never knowingly hurt anyone. In fact, he had gained an enviable reputation of helping friends and acquaintances in need. He often surprised those who were down in political or bureaucratic setbacks with the same attention and consideration that he had given them when they were in ascendancy.

Now and then Bwana would muse about his good fortune. There were people who were cleverer than him or often worked harder, yet they had far less money than him. Was it luck? But then luck often favours those working smartly for it. This he had done. What, if he lost all his money? It would be a very sorry life but he won't commit suicide. He would live with it and try to rise again. Money was real power and he couldn't envisage living without it.

10 Udai Marries Raminder

On one of his visits to Delhi to see a polo match Sarabjeet happened to be introduced to Lt. Gen. Kuldeep Singh, an avid promoter of the polo game. Kuldeep Singh was once brigadier general at Jalandhar, the same post that Brig. Gen. Dyer of the notorious Jalianwala massacre had held. Later he shifted to army headquarters as major general and now stood elevated as lieutenant general. In the follow-up evening party, Sarabjeet was presented to the general's wife and his daughter Raminder.

The college-going girl was simply an eye-catcher, tall, athletic body, with dimples in her cheeks when she smiled, and merry dark eyes twinkling with fun. The thick crop of black hair reached down to her behind. Sarabjeet, a widower with twin daughters, almost fell in love with the attractive Sikh girl within minutes of talking.

To Sarabjeet it was love at first sight. He had never felt something like this before, not even for his pretty Durga Devi. On return he confided in Udai, his buddy, as to how charmed he has been with the lovely Sikh girl. "You would experience the same when you see her," he said, "I have asked the general to stay with me when he and his family happen to visit Jaipur next."

"I look forward to seeing the girl," said Udai, "Maybe I can make her marry me. To be frank, I'm sorely in want of a beautiful wife."

"I wish you the best of luck."

A month later Sarabjeet threw a large dinner party for the general and his family who, however, was not staying with him but at the army guest house. There, Udai saw Raminder and was similarly bewitched by her looks, manner of speaking, and the way she carried herself. No sooner than the guests left did Udai confide in his friend, "I would love to spend all my life with her. She is really something exceptional."

In time Udai wangled a posting as ADC to Gen. Kuldeep Singh. That gave him ample opportunity to see Raminder nearly every day. Udai was a star polo player while the general and his daughter were noted polo fans. Raminder herself was a confident, competent rider, a good jumper. She even joined men sometimes at polo play.

Udai as ADC to her father came into closer contact with Raminder. And this in turn developed into a tempestuous love affair. The couple would sometimes manage to slip on his motor-bike and take a walk in the well-kept Lodhi Gardens. They could sit there in relative privacy surrounded by greenery and the chirping of birds in trees. Thereafter, they would often go to Machan, a restaurant in Taj Hotel, for coffee and snacks. Udai would press his plea for marriage to her. Raminder's response would be a smile but no firm commitment.

After months of courting by Udai, her hesitation wore down. He would tell her of his plans for a career in one of the best regiments in the Indian army. Gave her details of his family, his notable lineage, and the ancestral property. Being the eldest of the three brothers, he will be entitled to his full share of the vast estate. In due course, Raminder became as keen for marriage to him as he was and began yielding to his embraces and kissing.

Soon Rammi broached her parents about her inclination to marry Udai. Rammi's mother was in favour of her daughter marrying a kesadhari Sikh, preferably from the IAS rather than the army.

"Army men," she said, "get posted to all sorts of outlandish places—at times, to places where their families can't join. You know how many times you had to move in your military career, and how long I had to live on my own. Anyway, army life is dangerous."

"Ours hasn't been too bad a living."

"The charm of army life is declining while that of civil services is on the rise. Nothing equals being the wife of a Deputy Commissioner, with all that power and prestige."

"I'm neutral. You better argue it out with Rammi. The two young persons are genuinely in love."

Rammi was adamant. She would marry none but Udai. And eventually the general sided with the daughter.

"Udai belongs to a notable Rajput family, had good education, and is posted in a premier army regiment. He is sure to go high in his profession," explained the general.

By this time Raminder had graduated in commerce from Lady Shri Ram College.

It came to a glamorous marriage; the couple so handsome, the arrangement so grand, and all those top army brass present. The actual marriage ceremony was conducted in a gurdwara. This was followed by a very impressive evening reception and dinner at the Army Club.

Sarabjeet, Udai's buddy, was his best man at the marriage; a situation where both the bridegroom and his best man were in love with the bride. Sarabjeet would have loved to marry Raminder himself, being smitten with her looks and personality the moment he saw her. Yet he did concede that Udai was a better choice; at least he was not burdened with an earlier marriage and the twin girls. Bwana may be richer but Udai was younger. And in any case the couple seemed to be madly in love.

After marriage Udai moved back to his regiment at Jaipur. Within a year, a baby girl was born. Simran remained the only child the couple was destined to have. A subsequent miscarriage resulted in a host of gynaecological complications. She and Udai flinch at the prospect of undergoing such an ordeal again. In due course Udai firmed up his plan to go for vasectomy.

11 Twins in Their Teens

The twins reached sixteen.

Shanti emerged a beauty. At five feet seven, she got her father's height and mother's delicate features. What struck one most about her were the high cheek bones, lush lips, and prominent dark eyes. And she possessed the most amazing hands, well-nigh perfect—hands that hadn't known any manual work or even serious sports activity.

Shanti primed and preened herself a long time before the full-length mirror in her room, as she dressed stylishly in salwar-kameez, sari or skirt. She did last-minute ironing even to laundered clothes. She was particularly vain about her hair; black, long, and lustrous, she mostly tied it with a ribbon at the back.

Shanti was the one who helped Bwana run the household. She had a regular discussion about it with the father every morning. And she handled his money needed for everyday expenses. She went about as if the mistress of the house.

Of the twins, she had been behaving in ways more responsible and more modest. And once when she did stray, her sister had something to do with it.

Kranti didn't bother much about her clothes or looks. She was growing a bit plump though quite active in games and riding. And she had gone for shoulder-length bobbed hair, strands of which kept coming on her forehead. An inch shorter to Shanti, Kranti was well built; gave an impression of being tough.

Raju drove the silvery Volvo van. He was rated a careful driver. A muscular, medium-height, 28, he dressed nattily in safari suits with a matching cap. He shaved regularly and kept a trimmed moustache. Yet you could not help noticing a certain coarseness in his facial features as found in one who smoked too many bidis and cheap cigarettes. He was married but never brought his wife and children to town. They lived on the family land somewhere near Nainital.

Raju's job was to ferry the twins to school, to sports, and other activities, such as shopping. And this he had been doing so for six years. Kranti went out more often; she played badminton matches and represented her school in girls' volleyball.

By fourteen, Kranti, the tomboy, came into full-fledged puberty. She was grappling with a surge of hormones. She had developed biggish breasts that drew particular notice among her classmates. She believed her big breasts were a gift of God. Even let a couple of boys rub these as if "accidentally". At twelve, she had started wearing a bra, a year before her twin sister whose little buds took their own time to develop. Kranti was filling up fast at the hips, acquiring almost a woman's body.

She played with herself in bed and in bath. Occasionally, she shaved her pubic hair. She began to sit in the front seat when being driven alone by Raju. Flirted with him.

One evening, while returning home from a badminton game, she directed Raju to drive the van towards the back of the family farm. She actually had the premeditated audacity to take the ride in a skirt, with her panties off; she had stuffed these in her school satchel. Egging him on wantonly, she got rid of her virginity in the rear seat of the van while still a few days to fourteen.

"I'll tell you something if you swear to secrecy," said Kranti one night after dinner when Shanti came in to seek her help in doing a math sum.

"When have I babbled about you?"

"This is serious. You must swear in the name of what you hold most dear, the Dad."

"Alright, I swear."

"I did it with Raju this evening. Got rid of my virginity."

"My God! So shameless of you."

"It's my choice."

"Why that fellow Raju? Why not someone smarter?"

"What does 'smart' have to do with it? I wanted to lose my virginity, and Raju was handy."

"You're the daughter of a man held high in society. You can't behave like a slut."

"I did it and that's the end of it. Now, you keep your mouth shut."

"You could get pregnant."

"I made him withdraw before coming."

"I had no idea you knew all these things."

And the two remained silent for some moments, Kranti looking vacantly at her book, Shanti at the ceiling.

"How did it go? Did it hurt?" Shanti queried in a conspiring tone.

"You'll find it for yourself someday."

"Come on. Tell me how it went."

"Hurt like nothing had ever hurt before. But the worst is over. It is said to be smooth sailing thereafter."

Shanti getting up to go, "You've done a very wicked thing. God will punish you."

"I care a damn about God. Only don't tell Dad."

"Haven't I sworn to it? To be frank I feel like telling Dad."

"Some of my friends are doing the same thing. You don't mature without this experience," she said, outrageously, "but if you mention anything about it to Dad, I'll deny it outright. Nobody would believe you. And I shall never confide in you again."

"Anyway, stop this Raju business."

"Rest assured. I won't use Raju any more. His job is done."

"You're shameless."

"I'll do what I like."

"Better mend your ways. You'll land in trouble."

Only a week before, Shanti had come upon some pictures of couples mating stark naked, while rummaging through Kranti's home desk for her borrowed pen. She was simply shocked.

"You're seeing such naughty stuff, such filthy stuff," she accosted Kranti with it.

"Oh! These are a few reprints from Kamasutra. They're currently making the rounds among three of my girl classmates."

"You'll be in serious trouble if Dad comes to know of it."

"It's only a harmless peek, a bit of fun. What about this one, with a man doing from behind?"

"No, I don't want to see it," Shanti said, putting her hands over her eyes.

"That's up to you. By the way, I'll be returning the pictures tomorrow."

Raju, it appeared, got a taste of it. He was terribly keen to have more of the same. Tried persistently but was roughly rebuffed. Kranti behaved as if nothing had transpired between the two of them.

In time, Raju diverted his attention to Shanti. Once he made her hand casually touch the rise in his trousers. To his pleasant surprise, she didn't give him black looks or shout at him.

By seventeen, Shanti also lost her virginity to the rascal.

Whereas in the first case, Kranti took the initiative, it was Raju who had to do a lot of coaxing with Shanti.

Once, the twins had shared a womb. Now they shared the same deflowering tool. The gardener Mellors in Lawrence's *Sons and Lovers* had bedded only the lady of the house. Our local Mellors notched a double of his employer's virgins.

Presumably Raju's loose talk ruined him, not anything emanating from the twins. A garbled version of what was happening reached Bwana's ears. One line of action that suggested itself was to horsewhip the rogue and boot him out. The other was to offer him the inducement of money to quit the town quietly and never return. Bwana opted for the second alternative, not because he wasn't itching to thrash the bastard, but because it would minimize scandal.

Momentarily, Bwana wondered whether he could possibly find a woman driver for the twins. He could get one if he tried hard. But that could become a joke with the city and give undue publicity to the wayward ways of the twins. So he opted for a driver of over fifty, known for good behaviour.

Rajpal, the trusted assistant, called in Raju. "Here are rupees ten thousand, a sum you definitely don't deserve and you're unlikely ever to earn. Leave Jaipur this very night and never return. If you're seen again, it would invite reprisals you'd rue for a long time."

Making a quick grab for the bundle, the bastard whined, "On my mother's oath, my lips will remain sealed. And I won't ever enter Rajasthan, what to say of Jaipur."

"Good. Now get out. I don't want to see your bloody face any more."

Raju couldn't complain of a raw deal. He got a windfall of ten thousand rupees and two high-end maidenheads.

Bwana has learnt a lesson. In the absence of their mother, he has to play the role of both parents more effectively.

Reprimanding the twins for their misdeed, he thought, wouldn't serve much purpose. The girls in all probability would deny it vehemently and proclaim their innocence. The situation actually called for closer supervision and watch over their activities. The spinster Nirmala, working as a housekeeper, was evidently not up to the mark in keeping watch over the girls. She was too low in education, personality, and status to impress and direct the ebullient twins.

So, Bwana soon selected another lady housekeeper whose primary function would be the care of the twins, more so in keeping an eye on them. And she was someone known to have a hawk's eye and an uncanny supervisory skill. Prabha, a presentable 36-year-old, had worked as a superintendent in a girls' hostel.

It didn't take much time for Prabha to realize that, of the two, Shanti required little of her services. At best it meant giving her company in shopping for clothes and some assistance in studies. In time, they became more of friends than a chaperone and the chaperoned.

As to Kranti, the situation was getting more complex. Prabha was hard put to keep a track of Kranti's movements and doings. And who knew that this could well end in an ugly situation.

12 Bwana Eludes a Marriage Trap

Of the twins in the school, Kranti continued academically at the top of her eleventh class (the last year of her secondary class). On the other hand, Shanti was found labouring in mathematics and economics. She seemed to lack the concentration called for.

Bwana favoured a private tutor to make up for Shanti's deficiency, and the choice finally fell upon a lady lecturer of the Maharani College for Girls. Miss Sarla Kapur was known to be a good teacher in the two subjects. So it was arranged that Sarla would coach Shanti for about two hours every Sunday, followed by joining the family at lunch. That would give Bwana an opportunity to know of the progress Shanti was making.

Sarla Kapur was not only a top tutor in the subjects, she happened to be a presentable woman around 28, with prominent breasts and buxom hips. She had a pair of inquisitive eyes. The only jarring feature was a bit of flat nose and larger than normal ears. Yet she made full these deficiencies with a tall body and firm steps. And she had almost a European complexion. The bobbed hair falling on her shoulders, swayed provocatively whenever she moved her head. Bwana came to learn that Sarla was from a well-to-do Punjabi family of Kapurs who had settled at Ajmer. The family had a wholesale liquor business and an outlet for sale of guns, the business being looked after by her father and elder brother. A younger brother was in the merchant navy.

During the leisurely lunch Bwana could not help noticing Sarla's coquettish ways. She appeared fairly flirtatious. It was fun having her at lunch. It's another matter that Sarla and Raminder didn't hit up well whenever Raminder happened to be present at the lunch.

One day, Sarla rang up Bwana, "My merchant navy brother is here for a day. Could you join us at dinner tonight?"

"Why don't you both come to my place for a meal," Bwana said in response.

"It will give you a chance to see my flat," said Sarla, "I shall cook a special meal for the two of you."

"Alright, I'll be there around eight. Please give directions to my driver Balwinder."

Bwana was there in time with a bouquet of red roses and a bottle of Black Label. The meal went off well. Her brother turned out to be a jolly fellow who enjoyed his drink. He regaled the company with stories of visits to foreign ports. Asked when he plans to marry, he said "Sailors don't make ideal husbands. Anyway, marriage for me is some years away."

"Sailors, I'm told, have a wife at every port," said Bwana, and this produced a laugh.

Bwana found Sarla's flat on the second floor in an uptown area quite spacious and in a good shape. Plenty of books could be seen everywhere. When she came down to bid Bwana good night, she snuggled into his arms and pouted her lips for a possible kiss. Bwana held back. A kiss did not materialize; it takes two to kiss.

A month later, Bwana got another telephone call from Sarla, "Could you come for dinner on any day this week? I know you have a busy social schedule."

"I shall ring back," said Bwana. He was in half a mind to wriggle out of the invitation. He could see that Sarla was angling for sex and marriage. And this was not right with him.

Getting no positive answer for a week, Sarla reminded Bwana, "I eat so many times at your place. Let me return some of that hospitality." After a few moments, Bwana responded, "Alright, I shall be there the coming Saturday."

Bwana was driven to Sarla's place; he had ultimately agreed to her persistent invitation. He carried with him a huge bouquet of flowers and a bottle of chilled Brut champagne. Sarla was there in a thin silken dress, the pink blouse with a low neck, and a matching skirt. The blouse managed to show a good bit of her cleavage.

The two settled down to a nice chat, with a plate of almonds and pistachio kept in front. She was for offering whisky with soda. Bwana persuaded her to go for the bubbly. He opened the bottle with the cork popping up a few feet. Sarla was delighted with this popping up novelty.

Bwana poured a generous glass each. Being a moderate drinker, Bwana was going slow with his drink but Sarla, liking the sweet taste of the champagne, kept on refilling her glass. Indeed, she was drinking champagne as if it was lemonade, quite oblivious to the fact that unlike wine, champagne imparts a special kick. Within an hour she was as good as drunk and unmindful of the waiting dinner. Sarla propelled him into her bedroom on the excuse of showing him her recent collection of books. He saw a large double bed, a bit incongruous for single occupant. Evidently it was meant to accommodate more than one body.

After a frantic phase of hugging and kissing, Sarla made him sit on the bed. Excusing herself for a few moments she went into the adjoining bathroom. There she took off all her clothes and saw herself in the mirror. In fact, in the early evening itself she had shaved her pubic hair, bathed and perfumed herself in the same place, let alone brushing her teeth again. She believed she had a voluptuous body, a body that could turn on most men. Sarla was sure Bwana would fall for it on getting a full view.

There she stood with her bosom bare, an attractive light cream pair with the little nipples erect. To the sex-starved Bwana, the comely nude figure was proving too much. As they embraced, Sarla had the audacity to put his hand on her moist patch.

Within minutes, the two lay naked in bed for fast, furious sex.

In time, they were back into their clothes, eating the dinner, mainly of fried fish and later caramel custard. And soon after, Bwana left for his place.

During the next few weeks, Bwana had several telephone calls from Sarla for coming to her place again. He, however, put her off on one pretext or the other. With the coming of the exams, her teaching assignment with Shanti had ceased.

It had been no more than two months since their sexual encounter when Sarla rang up, "I'm pregnant. Missed two periods. Please do come soon. We have a lot of things to talk about."

This came as a thunderbolt to Bwana. He never envisaged this complication from a single unintended sex act. Pity, he failed to use a condom. Of course, he will provide for the child, even the mother, but there was no question of his marrying her—he was in love with Raminder. This complication of Sarla's pregnancy did bother him a great deal. Should he counsel her abortion?

Bwana told Sarla that he would soon be coming to meet her. Meantime, he arranged a special informant to make enquiries about Sarla's character and whether there was any other man in her life. He learnt that Sarla was carrying on with a married colleague in her department.

Bwana consulted Adoor, his doctor friend and confidant. Adoor advised that we should have a DNA test of the paternity of the unborn child before mapping out any strategy. Adoor, however, admitted that it was quite complicated to get the DNA of a baby in the womb. "I've a reputed gynaecologist friend Dr. Sinha. He can do the job in secrecy provided you persuade the lady to consult him."

Sarla kept on asking Bwana to meet her. He in turn suggested that she might come to his place. Sarla did come and the two sat in his office-cum-library. The door was closed. As she sat, Sarla blurted out, "I'm now carrying our child for over two and a half months."

"Have you thought of abortion? I can arrange and pay for it."

"No, I don't want to abort. This is a precious product of yours and mine. In the circumstances, marriage is the only option."

"Sarla, please understand my position. I'm in love with another woman. Ours will be a loveless marriage."

"Many of our marriages start loveless. Love develops later on."

"You may be right. But I've been in love with someone for over ten years."

"You mean Raminder, the wife of Udai! That's the talk of the town."

Sarabjeet's response was a studied silence.

"In any case, please have a check up. I shall fix an appointment for you with Dr. Sinha, a reputed gynaecologist."

"I can meet him as you suggest, though it does not seem really necessary."

Dr. Sinha, under instructions from Dr. Adoor, not only carried out a routine check up but did manage to get the child's DNA. It turned out incompatible with Bwana's. The child was evidently sired by someone else.

This information took off a load from the shoulders of Bwana. He was not a party to the conception of an illegitimate child. Bwana, however, had sympathy with Sarla in spite of her manipulation.

On her next visit, Bwana told Sarla that the unborn child was not his as proved by a DNA test during her examination conducted by Dr. Sinha.

Sarla flew into a rage. She shouted back, "The DNA test must be wrong. Who else could be the father?"

Bwana retorted, "A DNA test is never wrong. Yet I agree to support the child and the mother, if necessary. But my marriage to you is out of question."

Sarla ranted, "You are in love with a married woman. It's shameful enough. The whole town knows of it. And now you disown me and your child. What sort of a man are you?

Bwana kept his cool. He could appreciate Sarla's point of view. She was hoping for a marriage with a rich man. She dreamt of living in the luxurious Devi House, the one she had been frequenting for some months. She would have been using Bwana's money, a commodity most versatile. And now her dream-scheme was in shambles. She got up abruptly from the office chair and shouted, "I'll take revenge for this ill-treatment. I'll expose you to the whole world. I would even approach Udai about it. I'll not let you live in peace."

Bwana had nothing to say as Sarla hurried out. Sarla had reasons to be angry. She considered herself beautiful with an enticing body, and she could be very pleasurable in bed. Again, Sarla liked Bwana, his manners, his powerful body, and his good looks. She had almost fallen in love with him. She was sure that as a wife she would give him full satisfaction and in turn she would have access to all his money; money that meant luxurious living, a great wardrobe, lots of jewellery, and travel to exciting places. All in all, the feel of power that money brings.

True to her threats, Sarla did start a campaign of vilification against Bwana. She even tried to meet Raminder. The latter refused. Raminder had some idea as to what had happened.

In Sarla, Bwana presumably was having his worst enemy. Meanwhile, she quietly opted for an abortion at Delhi. Learning of it, Bwana sent through Rajpal a sum of rupees one lakh for the abortion expenses. Sarla took the money but kept railing against Bwana.

Raminder could easily taunt Bwana about this affair. Yet she chose to remain silent about it. After all, Bwana was young and sex-starved for years. And she also assumed that Sarla was a clever manipulator. Indeed, Raminder was appreciative of the restraint Bwana had been showing in sexual flings, despite being rich and attractive. As to Udai, he laughed the whole matter off.

The two friends were together at drinks late one evening. "You ran into a real tough customer in Sarla," said Udai.

"You are right. The lady was too clever for me."

"Yet I suppose the sex encounter was a real fun," mocked Udai.

"Yes, it was, though unintended. And it has cost me dearly. No more Sarlas for me."

"Better go for good paid sex, preferably out of Jaipur."

"I will keep your suggestion in mind," said Bwana. And the two got up.

Sarla became a bitter critic of Bwana, possibly the only critic who openly campaigned against him. She even went to the length of writing anonymous letter to him threatening more disclosures. Bwana would sometimes say that Sarla was the only enemy he had.

She didn't relent even after the polo accident which rendered Bwana a cripple. In fact, she kept on proclaiming that Bwana intentionally killed Udai to get at his wife. It was only with the passage of six years and her marriage to a middle-age city businessman that she stopped campaigning against Bwana. She had finally succeeded in cornering a moneyed man. As they say, there's a lid for every pot.

It's another matter that Sarla's episode sometimes cropped up as a private joke between Raminder and Bwana.

13 Kranti Trips Up

Kranti at twenty turned out vastly different from the tomboy image she had at thirteen.

Her interest in sports continued. She figured in the college badminton team. And she rarely skipped her morning ride. She had grown into rather a big girl, muscular and robust, while Shanti remained slim, willowy. Kranti, an inch shorter, had big breasts and solid thighs.

She had shifted dramatically from tomfoolery to serious studies. In the premier Rajasthan College, a co-ed institution, she was at the top of her graduate class in economics and English. She spent hours in the college library, read in bed late into the night. Bought plenty of books and rummaged her father's library collection for more reading.

Kranti had grown a little more careful about her grooming and clothes. Yet her heart was set on a professional career. Her ideal was an independent woman, running her own business. She had seen far too many high government officials at her father's parties to be enamoured of government service.

Marriage was nowhere in her scheme of things. And no children figured in it, too.

Whereas Shanti was mediocre in studies while exemplary in her social conduct, Kranti was clearly lacking in sexual probity. And if Shanti was having a steady love affair of the "innocent" variety, Kranti indulged more in what could be termed "one-night flings". Since Kranti had lost her virginity at fourteen to the driver Raju, she had sex with six men; no mean average of one new episode per year.

This included a bellboy in a Rome hotel, a classmate during a mountain college excursion, a Sikh syce at the farm, the brother of Shanti's best girlfriend, a country cousin at Tikam thikana when visiting for a family wedding, and her college's gym teacher.

She looked for the thrill of a new male body. Yet she was in no mood to complicate her life with a continuing love affair. No wonder she went for ones in the lower social order or those she wasn't going to meet again.

Ironically, all her sexual forays till now had taken place in the daytime, not at night. And these were of the hit-and-run variety, starting with hardly any preliminaries and ending as abruptly. No love talk, no foreplay, no after-play. She insisted on the use of a condom which she herself supplied. And she brooked no advances thereafter.

Lucky, Kranti had till now escaped being surprised in the act itself. Yet rumours kept floating about her promiscuity. And if you happen to gather a reputation for promiscuity, all sorts of fellows get encouraged. But then she could be awfully brusque and rude in rebuffing such blokes; she was a former tomboy.

The problem with this approach was that a man was always hoping for a lot more than just one encounter. How this lesson will be driven home to Kranti has yet to be seen.

What bothered her most was the reaction of her dad if he came to know about any of her shenanigans.

Her latest, no one would imagine, was a quickie with Nari Master, her sister's lover and would-be husband. At a large lunch party at the farm, she inveigled Nari into a bathroom. And they had a fast one, she half on and half off the marble slab over the wash basin, the dangling legs spread wide. Good that he was tall enough to reach her comfortably on his feet.

Maybe her curiosity was tickled as to what her twin sister was in for.

"Ritu tells me you had sex with her younger brother," said Shanti, as she entered Kranti's room. The latter was reading a book of John Updike's stories in bed.

"The bastard. Boasting of it."

"So, it's true! Doing it with a boy of 17, and that also the brother of my best friend," Shanti shrieked.

"It happened in a weak moment. But that was a year back. Never even had a word since then with the cad. And, between us, I can tell you, he's no good. Just a raw kid."

"Oh my God! You speak like a street girl. Such talk coming from the daughter of a highly respected home."

"A bit of fun now and then. It's not a crime. You remember Raju."

"Raju was a blunder. You won't believe I'm going on with Nari for a year. Nothing beyond a hug or kiss."

"Test him once, at least. He may be impo," she giggled, though she had a good idea of things below Nari's belt. She deemed her sister lucky. But had absolutely no intention to let Shanti know how she came to know of it.

"Don't talk nonsense," Shanti reacted sharply, "you're treading dangerous ground. With this sort of reputation, we'd be hard put to find you a husband."

"I don't want any. I'll stay single, go into business."

"Hope Papa doesn't come to know of your doings."

Kranti went back to her book, as if the discussion stood terminated. Shanti returned to her room.

And it was only a question of time before Prabha approached Bwana with the Kranti problem.

"Sir, as you're aware, Kranti is doing exceptionally well in studies. But her attitude towards sex and marriage can be a cause for worry."

"What happened?"

"Nothing in particular. I don't see her dating anyone on a regular basis, as I keep track of her movements. Yet all sorts of rumours are afloat of her being promiscuous. Santa, the Sikh syce of her pony, comes for mention and so also Hari, a school boy whose sister is Shanti's best friend."

"I had my own doubts, too. Step up your vigil. We'll send Santa away."

"I will, sir. My problem is that she doesn't confide in me. If I broach the subject, she clams up and is even rude at times."

"The girls grew up without a mother. We have to keep this in mind while judging and handling them."

Bwana's new car, the BMW3, had been delivered. Everybody was keen for a ride in it, more so with the hood down.

It was a cool September evening. Kranti was back from college.

"What about a spin in the new BMW?" he asked her.

"I'd love it."

"Hop in," he said, sitting at the steering wheel. This would afford him a good chance to talk to her in private.

He headed towards Tonk, a relatively less crowded road out of Jaipur.

"Papa, the car rides beautifully. And you are driving so carefully."

Bwana mostly preferred being driven, especially with the city's traffic so mixed and haphazard. Yet when he did drive a fancy car, he drove with an extra care and courtesies, as if to proclaim to the world his good fortune and good manners.

Kranti put out a hand to switch on the music system. He motioned against it. Music, he felt, would disturb the flow of their projected talk.

"I'm gratified at your commendable progress in studies. The way you're doing, you can after graduation go to Harvard or Wharton Business School."

"That's my idea, too. To do a management course from a top American school and then start a business venture of my own."

"You'd have my full support."

"Thanks, Papa."

The subject he wanted to broach was rather delicate. But he had to. A level empty stretch of road helped.

"Some people are saying nasty things about you. Hope, these are unfounded, untrue."

Kranti knew the feared confrontation with Dad was looming.

"I may have made a few mistakes in the past."

"Everyone makes mistakes. The sensible ones learn from these. At least don't repeat them."

"But, Papa, I'm different from Shanti. My goal is a business career. Marriage forms no part of it. And if I'm to live on my own, am I not entitled to a bit of fun now and then?"

"I imagine one can successfully combine a career with marriage. Anyhow, I'm not pushing you on to marriage. But you have to be mighty careful about your reputation. A bad reputation—and once bad, very hard to rectify—can even hurt a professional career, let alone creating a host of other complications."

"All I can promise is that I shall be more circumspect in the future."

"Good. And see that you don't hurt yourself."

Only once Kranti faltered after that conversation, and faltered badly.

To her horror, she found herself pregnant. She had missed two periods. It must be the Christian gym coach of her college with his taut muscular body. She had motored with him to her father's farm.

The sex was great, Kranti supplying a condom. And as they lay in each others arms in post-coital torpor, the man, a real stud, did another quickie, this time without a condom. Kranti knew it was a mistake but failed to resist in the heat of the moment.

She did manage to hide her bouts of sickness, but how long could she hide the pregnancy?

"Are you all right?" asked Shanti when she found Kranti skipping breakfast and sitting listless in her bed.

"I wish I was dead."

"What's wrong?"

"I'm pregnant."

"Pregnant! Are you sure?"

"Yes. I've missed two periods. And I get morning sickness."

"What about a test?"

"I've done it with a home kit. It's positive."

"My God!"

"Who's the man?"

"Our gym coach. We did it once with a condom. But he repeated within minutes without a condom, and I couldn't stop it. That was a terrible lapse."

"What now?"

"Don't know. I've to abort. No question of carrying the brat full term."

"We have to tell Dad. There's no way out."

"He'll kill me. Only recently he had cautioned me to behave more circumspect. And I had promised."

Shanti took her twin sister into her arms for comfort. They sat bunched for some time.

And then Shanti said, "I'll tell Dad in my own way. Let his anger come down before he meets you."

"That would help."

They hugged again.

Bwana took the news calmer than what the girls had feared. With summer vacation approaching, he escorted them to Pune for a month's holiday. And there he arranged an abortion for Kranti.

They were all back, without anyone knowing about it. He didn't even rebuke Kranti too much; he knew she had suffered enough and learnt a lesson the hard way.

Children are a blessing, but bringing them up can give rise to a host of problems, mused Bwana.

14 Shanti's Marriage

Shanti was now in the last year of her graduation. Academically staying undistinguished, she could pull through the final exam. And then join a post-graduate course in history at Jaipur itself, if nothing else like marriage came her way.

Meantime, she got smitten with the love of a Parsi ophthalmologist, bearing the name Nari Master.

Nari's elder brother, Adoor Master, was a professor of surgery in the Swai Mansingh Medical College and a spinal surgeon of repute. Thirty-nine, single, handsome, Adoor had a winning personality. No wonder, he featured regularly in Bwana's parties. The two were now good friends.

In fact, Bwana had quite a few friends among doctors. He liked talking to doctors who often held more realistic views on life than laymen. It wasn't so much the need for medical assistance that attracted him to doctors but their approach to various problems of health and the very business of living.

Nari, commonly accompanying his brother, was again a frequent visitor to Devi House. And during these social contacts, mutual attraction had cropped up between him and Shanti. Like his elder brother, Nari was tall, fair, athletic, and always dressed smartly. He prided himself on wearing stylish Italian silk shirts of which he seemed to have an ample supply. He sported short hair that showed to advantage his broad forehead and attractive face. But what struck one most about him was a pair of deep blue penetrating eyes. That seemed to have a power to look into others.

Nari had come up fast professionally. At thirty-six, he was the top eye surgeon in the city, specializing in retinal surgery. He had built a flourishing private practice.

Shanti and Nari managed to meet quite often. By now, she drove and had her own car, a Fiat 1100. A favourite rendezvous of theirs was the family farm where they could walk about and enjoy each other's company in relative privacy. The two had fallen madly in love. An early marriage was on their mind.

On the sexual front, Shanti wasn't yielding to anything beyond hugging and kissing. Her usual reply to Nari's importuning and pressurizing, "Anything beyond has to await marriage." And her sole sexual encounter till date—the deflowering episode with driver Raju—hadn't been terribly exciting. At times, Nari wondered whether her stiff resistance to his loving overtures stemmed from a sense of modesty or could she be somewhat frigid.

"I hear talk of Shanti meeting Nari Master," Bwana called in Prabha to his office.

"That's correct, sir."

"Why didn't you tell me? Why do you let them meet in private?"

"Sir, it's hard to stop a grown-up girl with her own transport. As far as I can make out, there's genuine love between them, not sex."

"Jaipur is a conservative place. Young men and girls aren't expected to meet in private. People talk."

"Sir, what if she tells me they are intending to marry?"

"I have my reservations to the match."

Bwana hadn't been idle all this time. He had set up a couple of trusty assistants to make searching enquiries about Nari.

The gist of the reported findings: Nari hails from a respected affluent Parsi family; father and mother both doctors in Ahmedabad. Affection is evident between the two brothers, and both earned high incomes. The only fly in the ointment: Nari has a pronounced weakness for women. He has had several affairs in the past. In one case a receptionist in Adoor's surgery had become pregnant by Nari. A sum of money, not disclosed, was paid for the abortion and buying the girl's silence.

A few days later, Shanti herself came up to Bwana's bedroom after dinner.

"Papa, I want a few minutes with you alone."

"Sure. Go ahead," as he lay reclining against a pair of fluffy pillows.

"I'm in love with Nari and he with me. We want to marry, and as soon as possible," while she sat on the bed by his side, rubbing his feet.

"Hmm, I had hopes of your marrying someone in our community, at least a Hindu."

"Does caste and community matter so much to someone as cosmopolitan as you?"

"Marriage is a complex union of two people. And it could get further complicated when the couple hail from different backgrounds, more so different cultures and religions."

"We'll manage such differences." And after a moment's hesitation, she asked, "Frankly, Papa, have you anything against Nari himself?" as she took his hands in hers.

"Nothing about his looks, health, education, work, income or family. His elder brother, as you know, is my close friend," he said, shifting uneasily in bed.

Edging near him, she asked somewhat sharply, "What's the hitch then? Why hold back your blessings?"

"Nari is known to have had a string of affairs, and that included even an employee." He didn't want to make a mention of the abortion.

"What do you expect from a full-blooded male up to his middle thirties? To stay virginally pure till he marries! He doesn't have any other affair as of now, of that I'm sure. Told me himself of a few former girlfriends."

Bwana was in no position to pass judgment, having his own long, known nearness to his buddy's wife.

"I wish it had been someone from our community and more established, say an IAS."

"You mean Vinod Khanna, the Collector of Jaipur. He's such a pompous bloke, let alone being two inches shorter than I."

"You can't ignore the fact that Nari is sixteen years older to you," he said, in a bid to give another turn to the discussion.

"That's correct. But he's fit and healthy, indeed very fit. And I'm in love with him."

"You can surely take more time to decide."

"The timing we leave to you. But he's the one I want to marry," she said, getting up abruptly.

October, 1982. Devi House was being spruced up, readied for the biggest celebration it had known. Shanti was to wed Nari Master, a marriage of two lovers. The Jaipur weather during October is neither warm nor cold; it's ideal for both outdoor and indoor festivities. And there's hardly any risk of rain.

Planning for the mega event started weeks in advance. It meant everyday discussions with relatives, selected friends, and staff. With no housewife in position, Raminder was roped in to play the most conspicuous part. She was virtually in and out the whole day, making suggestions, contacting people, supervising arrangements, and making purchases.

The bridal dress was going to be a flaming red lehnga worked extensively in gold thread, with matching kurti and ohrni. The city's foremost jewellers, the Suranas, were kept busy making various ornaments for the bride and others. Yet the most important item was a tiara presented by Bwana to Shanti. The three-carat exquisite diamond piece for the head belonged to his grandmother.

"Try it on," he said.

And she did, gushing with excitement.

"It looks so beautiful on her," everybody watching agreed.

"This tiara is a part of our family story. Take good care of it."

"I may have to keep it in a bank locker most of the time," said Shanti. And then got up and gave her dad a tender embrace, "I love you, Dad."

Let alone her special relationship with Sarabjeet, Rammi enjoyed an excellent rapport with Shanti. The two confided in each other, exchanged things, and talked for hours. Shanti genuinely believed that her father and Raminder were just close friends, with no element of sexual activity in it. To Raminder, Shanti was her main ally in Bwana's household. And this ally's hold might well weaken with her moving out on marriage.

Kranti was clearly hostile to Raminder. And she made no pretence of hiding her animosity to someone she thought was intent upon snatching away the affection of their father. On her part, Raminder was apprehensive that Kranti's role and clout would swell in the absence of Shanti.

"This is the first marriage in the family for a long time," said Sarabjeet, "No expense will be spared and no ceremonial skipped. It must be a grand affair, the talk of the town."

"Rajput marriages even otherwise are faulted for being too showy, too wasteful. You'd go beyond—turn the whole thing into a mammoth extravaganza," Kranti muttered.

"We've a chance to share our happiness with many others."

"Dad, it needn't be a money-guzzling show."

"What's money for? What could be better than spending it on dear Shanti's nuptials? Her mother, if alive, would have been delighted."

Kranti had no answer to it. But she did fret at the tremendous attention showered on Shanti, and the blatant display of a mind-boggling dowry. The latest item was a new red Mercedes 180. The idea was to send off the bride and groom in the shining car, gorgeously decorated for the occasion, with the vehicle itself given away.

"Papa, are you sure Nari is the best match for her?" she said, changing the subject.

"They're in love."

"He's sixteen years older, a man of the world. Shanti, in comparison, is an overgrown kid, I'd say."

"Yes, the age disparity is there. But Nari's well-established, handsome, and hailing from a respected family," he said, sipping his coffee.

"He could stray unless Shanti keeps a tight grip on him." Kranti knew how easy it had been to seduce Nari.

"Shanti is a loveable girl. She should hold him all right."

Kranti was well aware that, whatever her misgivings, the scene was set for a fabulous marriage. Yet she couldn't help having a bit of fun at her sister's expense.

"Marrying a man sixteen years senior. And a balding one at that," mocked Kranti when the two sisters were sitting together in Shanti's room after dinner.

"Nari's not bald," Shanti retorted.

"Thinning hair—soon he'll be bald like his brother."

"He has a beautiful head, a strong manly face. I couldn't care less about the lack of his hair. Baldies are said to be sexy."

"That's old wives' tale. By the way, have you given thought to what might transpire in bed?"

Shanti, knitting her eyebrows, disdained to reply. Surely she had given a good deal of thought to what will happen in bed, spending hours daydreaming of it. But she wasn't going to share the same with her catty sister.

"You sacrificed your normal girlhood to a lonesome father. Now you may be sacrificing your normal womanhood to a balding oldie."

"Stop it. And take my advice. Keep your legs together. Hold them tight."

In the one encounter with Nari, Kranti did carry the impression that Nari was no good in resisting women. But this was something she didn't want to communicate to her sister at this juncture.

The marriage ceremonials kicked off with the issue of invitation cards to some 300 people, both in India and abroad. A brilliantly designed, elaborate card was accompanied by a box of choice laddoos (specially prepared with desi ghee) and sent out in a filigreed silver bowl. Bwana busied himself following up the invitations with personal calls. Twenty rooms were booked in the Rambagh Palace hotel for outstation guests.

A week in advance, a ladies' sangeet party was held, enlivened by the presence of two professional lady singers. Raminder was the one orchestrating the rollicking event. The men folk, challenged to match song for song—some of these bawdy—soon beat a retreat. They would prefer to stand on the sidelines, drink scotch, and bandy jokes. Of the prominent men drinking, Udai was in the forefront. He had recently returned from UK on his three months' training course. The men later joined the ladies at the buffet dinner.

As was customary, arrangement for the bridegroom's party coming for the marriage ceremony were undertaken by the bride's side—things like a mount for the groom and the accompanying music. Sarabjeet secured one of the most majestic tuskers in Jaipur to carry the bridegroom, with the city's vaunted police band in attendance. While members of Nari's family constituted no more than a score, some two hundred of his friends and acquaintances joined in. Indeed, most people on the bridegroom's party were known to the bride's side, too.

Nari cut a dashing figure in his cream-coloured silk achkan and an Udaipuri pugree on the gaily decorated giant jumbo. Someone wise cracked, "What happens if the beast refuses to sit down?" A groom sliding down its tiny tail wouldn't be an elegant sight. And the beast lifting the bridegroom in its trunk and depositing him on the ground could present its own anxious moments. But the majestic animal did lower itself at the mahout's command. Nari came down a small ladder to the ritual of mutual garlanding between him and the would-be bride.

The actual marriage rituals were conducted in a glittering *mandap*. The orthodox Hindu rites went on for over an hour. Nari's side didn't insist on any Parsi ceremony, except for a magistrate to be at hand to register the marriage and issue the requisite certificate.

The next day Sarabjeet gave a garden lunch party at the farm to some four hundred where invitees greeted the newly wed.

Nari's brother held a dinner party that night at the Clarke hotel.

At the Tikam thikana, the marriage was marked by a massive lunch feast to people there. Clothes, grain, and sweets were distributed to the indigent.

In two days the couple was off in the new Mercedes to a week's honeymoon in Shimla. Nari insisted on driving; he didn't fancy a driver sitting along with them.

Only time will tell how the glittering marriage would fare over the years. The initial conditions seemed to be promising.

15 How It Goes with Kranti?

Kranti graduated in high first class, with a top position in the university in economics. And she managed to secure admission in one of the best business schools in the US, the Wharton School in Philadelphia. To her dismay the school didn't offer a scholarship or grant.

"Don't worry," said Sarabjeet, "I'll support you there."

"Thanks, Dad. Yet I'm determined to be on my own at the earliest. I'll take up some part-time work."

"Don't. Concentrate on studies. If I can spend so much on your sister's marriage, surely I should spare some cash for your education also. Indeed, I would go with you to the US and get you settled there."

The two spent a couple of days in New York doing sightseeing and then went to Philadelphia.

Admission formalities were gone through. She secured a two-bedroom furnished flat jointly with another classmate of hers, a Canadian girl. Their upscale block was a walking distance to the main Wharton School building. Her roommate had an Audi car.

In the beginning, Kranti sorely missed the bustle of her home, its comforts, and the attending staff. She had never cooked before, washed dishes, or vacuumed rugs. At times she felt like giving it all up and going back.

Yet soon the charm of the new place, its orderliness, the inviting riverside, the high standard of studies and facilities, and the freer social setup won her over. She had every intention of studying hard for the business degree and staying away from distractions like bingeing or dating. "Plenty of time for those things," she mused, once she had done her basic studies. Kranti also strove to slim down with diet control and an hour daily at the school's gym. She had taken to wearing western clothes, mostly pants suits or skirt and blouse.

She did well each term, coming to the notice of a noted professor. On completion of the business course, she landed an apprentice posting in American Express (Travel Section), New York. Her plan was to start her own travel agency in Jaipur, a travel agency that would specialize in catering to high-spending foreign tourists looking for exotic travel in Rajasthan and other parts of India. Her heart was set upon pursuing a business career. Marriage was nowhere in the picture. Even a love affair had to wait. She must first establish herself in the travel business. Till then it would be, at best, a discrete, infrequent, one-night fling.

Kranti's idea was to gain work experience in the US for something like five years. Manhattan was getting to grow on her. The one-room sky-high flat was quite close to her company offices. The pay was adequate, supplemented with remittances from her father. She had made friends. And she had been to quite a few excellent restaurants and Broadway shows, enjoying comedies more than musicals.

The polo accident on the last day of 1984 jolted Kranti out of her plans. Sarabjeet, suffering a serious back injury, had been hospitalized in the UK for nearly a year. He was back at Jaipur. Bwana had to rely on crutches and a wheelchair. And he was suffering from several other health problems. In this condition, Sarabjeet wanted Kranti to come back and be with him for nursing and support. Shanti, living in London, was in no position to come. She had just delivered a baby girl.

Kranti resigned her job with American Express, to the regret of her boss, and joined her dad in Jaipur.

In due course she set up her own travel agency, named Own Travels. She rented rooms in an office complex on the premier Mirza Ismail Road and made a start with a couple of assistants.

In time her business expanded. She hired a full complement of staff and moved into her own premises; the whole first floor of a modern commercial building on Mirza Ismail Road itself, bought for her by Sarabjeet. He also provided for high-end furniture and other equipment. Sarabjeet was all encouragement in his daughter's business venture. With such a start and Kranti's hard work, the travel agency was fast becoming a successful venture.

Kranti by then was fully entrenched as the mistress of the Devi House. She looked after the household and the farm, even helped her father in his business. Yet her first priority was to tend to the physical and mental health of her father whose life stood transformed from riding and polo to crutches and wheelchair. To be close to him, especially for any emergency at night, she moved to the bedroom suite adjoining her dad's first floor suite.

With the educational and work exposure in the US, Kranti was now an efficient, hard-working, and hard-driving manager-cum-executive. She began taking greater care of her clothes and general appearance befitting such a role. At office she mostly wore Western clothes, which now went well with her slimmer figure. From her American stay she had developed a liking for strong freshly-ground coffee, installing one Italian machine in the office and one at home.

She was reshaping the farm. With polo and riding activity declining, though she was a good rider herself, the polo ponies were sold off. Only a couple of riding horses were retained. Her emphasis shifted to income generation through farming a few exotic vegetables and fruits. Staff had been pruned, doing away with quite a few under-worked ones, and a professional manager brought in.

Bwana had been particular about the poultry in the farm, which included some twenty White Leghorn hens along with a couple of cocks. He liked the farm-fresh brown eggs, and would even send some to his friends, such as Udai and Dr. Adoor. What Kranti did was to do away with the two cocks. Bwana, learning of it, was a little disturbed. "Why did you do away with the two cocks?" he asked Kranti one morning. "They were such beautiful, spirited birds."

"The cocks were a nuisance. They fought among themselves. Woke up everybody with their morning crowing. And the way they mounted the hens, it looked like rape."

"You mean the poultry farm can run without them," asked Bwana.

"Yes," she replied.

"Hens will keep on laying eggs as before. And they will cackle merrily with no feeling of loss for the absent cocks. Indeed, it could be quite a pleasant female world where no males are present."

Bwana's response was a hearty laugh.

The recreational aspect of the farm, however, stayed intact. She even added the attraction of mini golf and a small theatre for showing films. Kranti often included the farm as a visiting spot in the itinerary of her select tourist groups, with special entertainment laid out for them in the form of Rajasthani folk dances.

And Kranti was busy streamlining operations of the main household.

Sarabjeet was delighted. "You've grown so self-confident, so competent in managing money and matters; it's as good as my acquiring a son."

"Why one has to be a son to be efficient, not a daughter? Dad, you're still sexist."

"I mean, I have a daughter who is both a daughter and a son. But I don't see any prospects of getting a son-in-law."

"There you're right. I have no plans of marriage. I want to lead the life of an independent, successful professional. I dislike being bossed, and most husbands behave bossy."

Sarabjeet was not pressing her on the marriage issue. He couldn't help mulling over the problems of Shanti's marriage—an ideal love marriage, if it were to happen at all.

With hard work, push, and smart moves, Kranti had succeeded in building up a unique travel agency that catered to high-spending foreign tourists, mostly American. These tourists stayed in hotels like Raj Vilas of Jaipur, Udai Vilas of Udaipur, or Amar Vilas of Agra, where a room for the day could cost 20,000 rupees or more, and you needed reservations months in advance. Indeed, her intervention was often needed to get a room on short notice in these places.

Kranti travelled frequently to the US, Europe, and Japan to renew contacts and secure business. She could also accompany a select group of foreign tourists to some places in India.

Kranti had somewhat sobered up on the sexual side. It was no longer anyone around for a one-time fling. She was far more choosy with whom she slept.

The latest was an affair with the manager of Raj Vilas, the fabulous Oberoi hotel where tourists handled by her mostly stayed. Work-wise, also, the two came in regular contact. And she had been sleeping with him, a forty-year-old Goan Christian who was separated from his wife.

Curiously, it was again a Christian—after the experience of the Christian gym coach and subsequent abortion.

It was an open secret. Everybody knew about it, including her father.

"I hear you're going out regularly with the Christian manager of Raj Vilas," Sarabjeet asked Kranti.

"That's correct. We're a good deal together for the last one year. Some of it is for business, some of it for fun."

"Do you two intend marrying? Waiting for him to get a divorce from his separated wife?"

"I'm not marrying him or anybody else."

"So, it's what I call a no-win situation."

"It may be an all-win situation."

"It's your life, Kranti, and I won't interfere with it. But I do feel that a settled married life has much to recommend itself."

"Dad, I know your views. All I can say: I'll keep it in mind."

Kranti knew that her relationship with someone good in bed and otherwise sophisticated and pleasant as a companion was far different from that between Sarabjeet and Raminder—where it was love for love, with a near absence of sex.

And it was not only her father who favoured her marriage to Jacob; Jacob himself was pressing Kranti for it.

"I'd be getting a divorce within three months," he told her one night after a great bout of sex in a Vilas unoccupied bedroom. "The time has come for you to accept my marriage proposal."

Jacob was well aware that in marrying Kranti, he wouldn't only acquire a sexy wife, successful in business, but she would inherit millions from her father.

"No marriage for me, my dear, not for five years at least."

"Any particular reason for the delay?"

"Nothing in particular. I'm just not mentally ready for it."

And there the matter had ended.

How long Kranti's current affair would last was hard to predict. With the absence of a permanent commitment and the regular use of the contraceptive pill, one party could lose interest in the other, seeking a fresher pasture. And such a party in all likelihood would be Kranti. She would get bored with a man quicker. Might go in for a more powerful pair of loins.

16 Shanti in England

On her marriage, Shanti shifted to Nari's place, only a mile away from Devi House. It was a compact two-storey bungalow in the popular 'C' Scheme, shared by the two doctor brothers.

The elder brother wanted to move out, leaving the whole house to the newly weds. Nari wouldn't hear of it. "No, we'll live together as before."

Eventually a compromise was reached. Adoor would take up the first floor and run his own kitchen. Nari and his bride would have the rest of the house and the well-kept front lawn.

This wasn't the ideal situation Shanti had envisaged. She was keen to keep a first-rate establishment that could be the envy of friends and relatives. This wouldn't be easy with someone else sharing the place. Yet she did succeed remarkably well in transforming her place into a bright, showy one.

Let alone the elaborate dowry stuff, she kept on bringing various items of household use from her parental home: carpets, choice furniture, paintings, glassware, curios. Even quite a few potted plants.

Bwana, whenever he became aware of it, was indulgent. Kranti was manifestly unhappy—dubbed it as pilferage, even downright robbery. But then she was off to the US for study and work experience.

Shanti was everyday at her father's home or farm, the spacious welcoming places with all their facilities and amenities.

She wanted her husband all to herself. With Adoor sharing the same house, a good deal of their social life became common, despite Adoor's keenness to respect the couple's privacy.

Nari's maternal uncle in London, a noted eye surgeon in Harley Street—the one who was instrumental in getting Nari do this specialization in UK—was here. He had come to attend a medical conference in Delhi.

"I'd be retiring by the end of next year. Would be crossing sixty-five. Nari, why don't you come and take over my practice? I've my own well-equipped consultation premises and I am attached to Moorefield Eye Hospital."

"Nari's doing well here. And he's now married to a Jaipur girl," said Adoor.

Nari was sorely tempted. Here was the best opening he could envisage. He liked the heady life of London. He would grow up professionally, even make more money.

"You'd love London," he told Shanti.

"But I'll be going away from my father."

"He stays in London every summer. Has a house there."

Shanti was of two minds. She'd miss her father's home and so also her friends. But then they'd have an exclusive establishment, and her husband entirely to herself.

Bwana was opposed to the move.

"I'm already feeling lonely with Kranti away in America. You want to go, too."

"It's a nice opening for Nari. He doesn't want to miss it. Anyway you're a regular visitor to London."

"It's for you folks to decide what you deem best."

Let alone more loneliness for him, Bwana harbours serious misgivings about the London move. He knew that Nari was a flirtatious bloke. More chances of his straying from the marital bed in London than in the conservative Jaipur.

Nari took over his uncle's practice. He had the same specialty as his uncle, retinal surgery.

The uncle owned a house near Oxford, a fine three-bedroom house with the backyard sloping down to the river. It had an excellent location and many comforts. The uncle, a childless widower, would be moving to his cottage in Wales. He offered Nari the house along with much of its furniture for sale on easy installments.

Nari agreed. All his problems of securing a place to work and a place to live had been taken care of so satisfactorily within months of his arrival.

Shanti liked the house and the view it commanded. Yet she'd have preferred to live in London, savour more of the city life. At least be near to her husband's place of work.

Nari had a ten-minute drive to the rail station, thirty minutes by train to Paddington, and another thirty minutes by taxi to Cavendish Place that adjoined his Harley Street surgery. He liked travelling first-class by train where he could read newspaper or professional literature. He, however, was not reconciled to the jostling and escalators of the Underground. Always took recourse to a taxi. And it was the same one hour and ten minutes on the return trip.

Nari was out in the morning by 8:00 a.m. and was back only by 7:00 p.m. That was his five-day routine. On Saturdays he could be visiting some hospitalized patients but that would be more of an outing. Often Shanti travelled with him to London for shopping, seeing a play, or eating in a fine Indian restaurant. To her Indian food was still the most appealing. Weather permitting, on Sundays Nari was out half the day for golf, a game in which Shanti showed practically no interest.

By now Shanti was pregnant.

17 Bwana in a Wheelchair

The horrific polo accident on the last day of December 84 changed the seemingly even tenor of several lives.

Raminder was rendered a widow. It will take the perky woman time to overcome her husband's sudden, most unexpected demise, the loss of husband she loved and was totally dependent upon. She must perforce reconcile herself to a single state with its inevitable component of loneliness, social downgrading, and financial stringency. She had again to shoulder the burden and responsibility of bringing up her daughter, educating her, fitting her for a career, and eventual marriage. Feeling keenly her own lack of a marketable skill, Raminder was determined that Simran shouldn't lack qualifications for a professional career.

Her elder brother, running a hosiery mill in Ludhiana, wanted the sister and Simran to shift to Ludhiana, a move enthusiastically supported by their mother. Her mother was by now a widow, her heavy-set husband dying suddenly of a heart attack one early morning.

Raminder was in no mood to leave Jaipur, the city she liked. And there was Bwana, a very welcome presence.

Simran opposed to leaving her mission school in Jaipur or the city itself for an unfamiliar place. She had grown up in Jaipur. Bwana, her favourite "uncle", lived there. Indeed, she was meeting him more often, coming closer to him—a development frowned upon by Kranti. To Kranti, Simran was nothing but a sort of Trojan horse for Raminder.

Admittedly, their present inner-city haveli was no patch on the former cantonment bungalow, a commodious, comfortable dwelling set amidst greenery. Simran's school now entailed a longish ride through congested streets. And there was a distinct fall in their standard of living; in the food they ate, the clothes they wore, and the entertainment they could afford.

Kranti had been recalled back from the US. She was the one assisting her injured father in day-to-day living and helped run the huge household with its elaborate scale of social activity.

Shanti's position in the Jaipur establishment was getting considerably weakened. She lived 5,000 miles away. What's more, Kranti in taking over the management of the Jaipur household was squeezing out the staff, the backers and favourites of her contending twin sister.

Adoor was not only Bwana's friend and brother of his son-in-law he was Bwana's doctor for the injured spine as well as his confidant. Adoor was called frequently, almost daily, for help and guidance. Besides being a highly regarded surgeon, he was a man of literature, widely-read in classics as well as modern fiction. That possibly made him a better doctor, with his heightened sensibilities and understanding of human suffering. He could appreciate all the more Bwana's anguish arising out of a disabled body; a body enviably fit and athletic at 40, now laid low from sheer bad luck.

Nari, engrossed in his work, had been drifting away from his brother. His contacts with Bwana were also shrinking. The two didn't meet often even when Bwana was in London. Evidently Nari was too busy with his burgeoning medical practice and the business of making money. He displayed a penchant for the good things of life: classy food, great wines, and pretty women.

Bwana was the one to experience the most drastic transformation in his life.

First, it was the physical part. He had lost the use of his legs with little hope of gaining any strength in them for support. He was reduced to the use of crutches in moving about in the house. But it had to be a wheelchair for longer periods inside or outside the house.

Here was a man who was a strong, athletic, and star sportsman now reduced at forty to a life in a wheelchair. He was not even sure whether his manliness was still intact. A few fervid attempts at masturbation had failed miserably. Presumably, his mind wasn't into it; the limpy organ stayed inert despite all that bruising. All this made Bwana suffer acute mental anguish, let alone physical pain and disability. At times, thoughts of suicide assailed him.

"Why not swallow fifty Valiums and die peacefully in bed?" Yet there was his love for Raminder. He had to look after the welfare of his twins and even that of Simran. For him, suicide was out.

In social parties, people had to bend down to talk to him, whereas in the past they used to look up to his towering figure.

Bwana had also acquired a walker as well as a pair of crutches. Both required him to undergo the needed training.

He commonly woke up in the middle of night, accompanied by a feeling of utmost unease. At this point he had to swallow a sleeping pill. After trying various pills, he had come to rely on Valium. Valium helped him calm down and go back to sleep. And no day passed without his popping a painkiller. Even otherwise, his daily dose at breakfast had half a dozen different coloured pills: vitamins, pain relievers, steroids. He wondered how all these interacted with one another in his gut.

On some days he simply stayed in bed, daydreaming or reminiscing over his past, watching TV mostly news or games. He was deeply interested in political and other news, and fond of watching football, cricket, tennis and golf, besides horse races and show jumping.

It came to getting up only for the obligatory exercises, meals and visitors. Lack of physical activity was making him put on weight; more so with the heavy dosage of steroids whipping up his appetite. Even otherwise, he was a hearty eater.

"Your best bet is a lot of swimming," said Adoor. "Swimming will strengthen your upper body, and it does not hurt the back the weight of the body being taken up by water."

"Yes, I do swim in the afternoon every day. And you wouldn't believe that my two poodles jump into the pool as soon as they see me getting ready for the swim. Poodles are said to be water dogs. It's fun seeing the two dogs swimming nicely or playing with a rubber ball."

"Take out a new bottle of Royal Salute," Bwana told Hari, his man-servant, as he and Adoor sat down for an evening drink.

Bwana opened the silvery cork of the blue porcelain bottle, and poured out the golden liquid. As the two men lifted glasses, Bwana mumbled, "Pity, Udai's not with us. He'd have loved this Scotch. What great times we had together!"

Sarabjeet had never felt so lonely, so depressed before. Shanti was away in London. She was busy settling in the new place and was in a stage of advanced pregnancy. Udai was dead and Raminder was now an infrequent visitor. A little liveliness erupted when Simran amused him with her girlish talk.

Bwana had hundreds of friends and acquaintances. And he still did collect quite a few of them at his parties. Yet his sense of loneliness rarely left him.

The last day of December 84 had indeed turned out to be a terrible day.

18 Break-Up of Shanti's Marriage

Shanti's marriage was beginning to show signs of strain.

The conjugal bond had begun blissfully at Jaipur. And it continued to be so in the early phase in England. Nari was loving and considerate, as well as doing great professionally. Within five years of their coming to England, he built up a highly successful practice, both in terms of reputation and earnings.

Nari was lucky to get a good start through his uncle. On top of that he added his singular surgical skill, coupled with charming bedside manners. The way things were developing, Mr. Nari (now Mr. to his patients; leading surgeons are addressed as Mr., not Dr.) could be a top eye surgeon as well as a millionaire.

The surgery-cum-office on Harley St., which had been given by his uncle, was a great help. In the prestigious street, it contained a nice reception room, a spacious consulting room with a work table in the middle, a high examination bed on one side, and all sorts of equipment therein. In the connecting room sat his secretary, while in the next one was an office with an accounts clerk and a cashier. The whole place was tastefully furnished and well kept.

The operating part he performed at the Moorefield Eye Hospital where Nari functioned as a premier consultant.

Shanti revelled in the rising tide of riches. She could buy what she fancied, and she liked shopping in high-end stores, especially in Knightsbridge. She could give full vent to her keen ambition to have a house that would be the envy of friends and neighbours. They could afford a full-time live-in maid. Nari presented her with a marine blue BMW3 on her 25th birthday, a replacement for her Toyota Corolla.

And they had been blessed with a baby girl, though Shanti had hoped and wished for a boy. It was a beautiful baby, mostly smiling.

"We'll name her Alka or Aarti, the A of her father's esteemed brother, Adoor," said Shanti.

"These are purely Hindu names. She should have a Parsi ring to her name," countered Nari.

The debate went on for days, till they settled on Nargis, a name that was neither Hindu nor Parsi.

Shanti wanted another child, a boy. To Nari one child was enough, and he didn't care particularly for boys.

Bwana was in London for an appointment with his surgeon. Life was hard for him; he felt bound to his wheelchair. His back still bothered him. In the house, he mostly used crutches. Yet he managed to watch polo matches and be present at some horse races, duly helped by a male attendant and a specialized car that took in the wheelchair. He liked playing with pretty Nargis whenever visiting Shanti. And it was fun for him in getting Nargis and her mother to his place.

One morning, Shanti had come to him driving all the way from Oxford.

"Where's Nargis?" Bwana asked when Shanti stepped in.

"She's at school."

"Not much schooling going on at six. You could have brought her."

"I've come for a serious talk with you."

"Go ahead. Is there any problem? By the way get yourself a cup of coffee and also give me one."

Shanti coming back with coffee and a plate of biscuits and chocolates, said, "Papa, I've a feeling Nari is carrying on with someone."

"Are you sure?"

"Almost. He does his marital functions in bed but it looms more like duty than fun. Some one-night fling or call-girl stuff I always suspected. But this looks different. I think it's his secretary, Eve Holding, a divorcee of 30. Two times when I rang him up, he and Eve were out lunching, out for a couple of hours. When out at lunch, he switches off his cell phone."

"Have you met Eve?"

"Only once at the office. She's a youngish-looking sexy blonde, a little on the plump side, more like Kranti than me. Keeps her hair tied in a pony-tail and has a very pleasant way of talking. She doesn't use much makeup, yet presents an attractive face."

"This needs looking into."

"Dad, I'm some fifty miles away from his surgery. Can't keep track of what happens there."

"Have you talked to him?"

"Nothing in the way of direct accusation. Only dropped hints now and then."

"Hmm," Bwana straightened himself in the chair, and put down his coffee cup.

"I don't want to bother you with all the details, but I've been doing my best to keep him to myself. Have been taking extra pains to make myself appealing in bed and otherwise. Even worked on the theory that plenty of sex at home discourages philandering. Nothing seems to work. He has been throwing hints that I am getting frigid. But, papa, this is not correct. Yet I can't cooperate with him in bizarre sexual practices—things like anal sex. I think he simply craves variety in mates; an incorrigible womanizer."

"I had feared something like that. I tried to dissuade you from your marital choice," he said as he popped into his mouth a piece of chocolate. Bwana was rather fond of top quality chocolates. He patronized a particular chocolate outlet in front of India House.

"Love had blinded me then."

"My speaking to Nari won't improve matters. However, I'll take up with my friend Adoor on return to Jaipur. If anyone, only Adoor can influence his younger brother."

"I'm planning to withdraw sexually from him till he fires his secretary."

"Such withdrawal often makes matters worse. And I'm doubtful whether he can straightway fire his long-standing secretary without a serious dislocation in work."

"So what can be done?" she moaned, tears trickling down her cheeks.

"Let us first be sure your suspicions are correct. We probably hire a detective agency to get an update on what our Nari is doing. I'll hire one. Let you know their findings."

"Thanks. That would help."

Shanti had one basic problem. She fell into the category of bored wives. When Nargis was small, mother-care took much of her time and attention. Nargis was now away to kindergarten for four to five hours. And no more children had been coming; Nari didn't want any.

Shanti had time hanging heavy on her hands. The initial enthusiasm to run a first-rate house was waning. She had no absorbing interests or hobbies; the piano start hadn't been followed up. And Shanti had no marketable skills. She hadn't even developed a reading habit to entertain herself in spare hours. How much TV could she watch, or go out for shopping, or talk to neighboring women? Their closest friends were the couple in the adjoining villa, and both were professors in an Oxford college. Shanti had hardly any women friends who were free during the day for chatting or shopping excursions.

All in all, Shanti hadn't put her mind to anything serious except being a tidy wife and doting mother. And she was getting into her late twenties. This realization was adding to her feeling of failure in life. Yet she didn't display the requisite willpower to take up anything meaningful.

This aspect of Shanti had even proved a disappointment to Nari. Off and on, he had been encouraging her to take up some studies or professional courses; they lived near Oxford, a centre of learning. Shanti would respond positively to his suggestions, such as doing a degree in business management, or doing fashion designing or simply opening a boutique for Indian clothes. She made plans but failed to follow up anything in a practical, concrete manner. Evidently, she lacked the staying power for these enterprises. Maybe, she had too cushy a girlhood. She had even failed to learn elementary work on a computer. She could neither send an e-mail nor receive one, not to say of doing any online business. She remained a computer illiterate despite Nari urging her to the contrary.

You could call it a flaw in her character; the incapacity and lack of stamina to carry out any complex business or educational project. This was a bit surprising because she was quite good in doing day-to-day activities, was a shrewd shopper, and seemed smart in managing money matters. Possibly, the main trouble was that Shanti lack an inquisitive mind, combined with inability to follow up an agreed programme with persistence.

The detective agency hired by Bwana did a brilliant job. Within a month, its report provided details of lunch-time lovemaking between Nari and Eve, commonly in her Portland flat. She was said to have a 9-year-old son living with her. And she had been putting pressure on Nari to divorce his wife and marry her. He didn't seem interested in any new marriage. The agency had managed to install a listening device in her bedroom and a hidden camera, too.

Surprisingly, all of Nari's lunch love-outings were not with Eve alone; he had also been with a few high-end call girls.

It was the day before Sarabjeet would be leaving for India. Nari and Shanti had invited him to dinner at their place. Nargis wanted to monopolize her grandpa. Nari was all fun and jollity. The men drank Glenlivet before meal, red wine with beefsteak, and Camus brandy with coffee. Shanti was simply entrancing in her silk sari.

It all presented a charming picture of a happy family in a beautiful, affluent home at a prize location. The view of the fast-flowing river from the terrace was enchanting.

Sarabjeet was not sure whether it was a good idea to end the marriage.

Next day, Shanti had come to see off Bwana at his place before he left for the airport. He showed her the report of the detective agency.

"Give it to me," she said. "I'll confront him with it."

"Maybe you'll get it later on. Meantime, I'd counsel patience. Give yourself at least one more year before any breaking off. I'll speak to Adoor. Could bring him along when I come to London next."

"Is it fair for Nari to behave like this?"

"There are all types of men. Surely, Nari has a weakness that's hard to accept but it is not so uncommon. He is evidently one of those who relish the very process of seducing women. Yet he has been a good father, a good provider, a good professional, and a good head of the house. He may mend. People sometimes change. I haven't given up all hope."

"What a hope!"

"And better divert your mind to something absorbing. Join a course in the university. If nothing else, give time to some social organization. What about doing voluntary work for the kindergarten where Nargis goes?"

This elicited from Shanti a tepid response.

Shanti's marriage continued to come under increasing strain. She was now convinced that her husband was an inveterate womanizer, an incorrigible. The report of the detective agency hired by her father had fully corroborated her misgivings.

At this stage, Bwana made one more attempt to salvage the tottering marriage. An obvious option was to put pressure on Nari to change his ways. Possibly, the last option for Shanti could be to bide her time with a straying husband, if otherwise Nari continues to be a good provider, a good father, and never nasty to her personally.

One day, Dr. Adoor had come for a thorough examination of Bwana's back. "You should be happy that your back is getting better."

"You mean it's getting no worse."

"I won't be surprised if with regular exercise you would get more strength in your legs."

"Leave this wishful thinking." and Bwana added, "Come for drinks by 7. I have to talk something serious about Shanti's marriage. We'll only be the two of us."

"Sure, I'll be there," Adoor said, though he had an uncanny feeling something unpleasant was in the offing.

As the two men sat in the Devi House bar (with cell phones off), Adoor with Glenlivet Scotch, Bwana with a glass of Chardonnay, the host began, "Shanti's marriage is in shambles. It is a development that makes me sad. Nari sleeps with his secretary Eve, and with others. I didn't believe it of Shanti till a detective agency hired by me confirmed it conclusively. Here's the report." And Bwana handed over the two-sheet document to him.

Adoor took his time reading it.

"It's bad. Nari had a streak of womanizing. Marriage, I thought, would put a stop to it. This hasn't happened, despite his marriage to a charming lady; a woman, he once told me, he was madly in love with." And Adoor continued, "I'll write to him, talk on telephone. He hasn't been much in contact with me for the last few years."

"Don't know whether this would do. Why not come with me to London the coming summer? You can talk face to face at length, see yourself how Nari functions. Maybe you talk to Shanti, too."

Adoor thought over it a bit.

"I can manage a week out in the first half of July."

"Good, we will go together."

"If you don't mind, I'll stay with Nari. It will also give me a chance to see the couple at close quarters."

"It's OK with me."

"I'll also fix an appointment with your spinal surgeon. We can discuss your case and the need of any further surgical intervention. Meanwhile, I'll assemble all your medical papers."

"Thanks. I don't know what I'll do without you."

Adoor had been staying with Nari and Shanti for the last three days. He was much impressed with the way Shanti managed her household; an exquisite taste in furniture and fittings, spotlessly clean premises, well-kept garden, an attractive room for Nargis, excellent meals, and his comfort being looked after in every detail. Nargis, he found, was growing into a charming girl.

The brothers were out for a short pre-dinner walk on the river bank. It was daylight at 8 p.m.

"Sorry to ask you a personal question," said Adoor. "How are things going between you and Shanti?"

"Has she talked to you about it? Or, you heard something from Bwana?"

"No, she hasn't talked to me. But Bwana is unhappy the way discord is developing in Shanti's marriage, a marriage he celebrated with much splendour."

"Shanti is suspicious about my relations with the secretary Eve."

"Has she valid grounds for her suspicion?"

"Maybe, I did have sex with Eve a few times. But that phase is over."

"Do I understand there is no woman in your life just now except Shanti?"

"I'd say none, not even Shanti," he said with a snigger. "She has discontinued marital sex for some months."

"All this must be operating a little hard on my sexy brother."

"I manage an occasional outlet, a one-night fling."

"Alright, are you prepared to fire Eve in the interest of marital harmony?"

"No. Not for the time being. She has been there for nearly 10 years and is almost indispensable in my work."

"Will you get rid of her within a year? That gives you enough time to find a replacement."

"I don't know. I can't promise."

"Do I understand, you're unwilling to do away with Eve, even when it is hurting your marriage?"

Nari failed to respond. He kept looking at a pleasure boat that was skimming past.

"It's not fair, Nari. Once you have had sex with someone, the presumption is that you'll have it again. How do you expect Shanti to reconcile herself with the continued employment of Eve? A wife may overlook an occasional one-night fling but she can't accept her husband spending virtually his whole working days with a woman with whom he had sex. Continuing with Eve would spell the end of your marriage."

"Give me some time to think over it. Maybe, I can persuade Shanti to accept the presence of Eve in the interest of my work."

As the brothers turned homeward, Adoor was constrained to remark, "Frankly, I'm disappointed in you. Are you thinking of a divorce with Shanti and marriage to Eve, a divorcee with a grown-up boy? Ruining Shanti's life and so also of that lovely kid, Nargis."

Nari answered with a shrug, "Your views carry weight with me. Give me some time to sort out the mess."

Next day, Adoor and Bwana saw Bwana's British spinal surgeon. After going through all the records and a prolonged physical examination, he didn't recommend any more surgery. "I'm not unhappy with your back. Continue with your exercises and physiotherapy. As to the use of your legs, unfortunately there is no near prospect of recovery."

The two friends adjourned to Café Royal, their favourite meeting place for a leisurely lunch.

"The news about your back is not bad," said Adoor as they waited for the meal to arrive. "But, Nari is a disappointment. I have a feeling he is presently more interested in Eve than Shanti."

"I was hoping he would listen to you."

"I get a feeling he is no longer interested in living with Shanti. Possibly, this was a mistake on her part to go off sex with him, but then she had every right to do so."

Bwana said with a sigh, "Shanti's marriage is over, a marriage on which I had lavished so much love and attention."

"Yes, it is sad. Maybe, Shanti can marry again. She is young and beautiful, and an excellent housewife."

"I don't think so. It looks like both my twins are destined to live with me; Shanti as a divorcee and Kranti as a spinster.

That makes for five females in their own different ways dependent on me; Kranti, Shanti, Nargis, Raminder and Simran. And me a cripple, with no legs and a bad back. It makes me wonder sometimes whether God is a female."

Bwana and Adoor were at their usual evening drinks.

"Shanti's situation worries me greatly," said Bwana, "It is neither reunion nor divorce. I suppose Shanti could have a new lease of life if she remarried; she is beautiful and a charming hostess. But if years pass on like this, she would be rather old for attracting someone suitable. Please understand that she has no professional skill and unlike Kranti, no aptitude for outdoor work. She's essentially a housewife, an ideal homemaker."

"I share your anxiety. A couple of times I rang up Nari to ascertain as to what were his future plans. Reunion or divorce! He gave no definite reply. Said, he was still thinking about it."

"It's already two years since Shanti had been here. How long can she wait?"

"I will take it up again with Nari. He must give us his definite decision within a month."

Adoor had quite a few long telephonic conversations with Nari. He pushed him to decide one way or the other. Nari kept on saying that he was not in any hurry to remarry. In fact, he has no one in view. But he was not willing to take Shanti back, at least for the time being.

Finally, Adoor persuaded him that he pay Shanti separation money till they are divorced.

"What should I pay as separation money?" Nari kept on asking, "I'm not as rich as you people imagine."

"I know your income and your expenses. You can easily give one million pounds over the next 10 years."

"One million pounds! Make it one or two hundred thousand."

Eventually it was agreed between the two brothers that Nari could pay Shanti half a million pound, to be given in ten equal annual installments. This would also cover all educational expenses of Nargis.

The two brothers also agreed that if Shanti and Nargis had no objection with the arrangement, Nargis could travel during her summer vacation to stay for two weeks with her father. He will be sending her a return executive class air ticket.

Next time, when Adoor met Bwana, he explained the situation.

"It looks quite fair," responded Bwana. "I'd consult Shanti and let you know our final views in the matter."

In due course, Shanti agreed. She would be a rich woman and nothing stopped her from divorce and remarriage if something came her way. Only the separation money will stop. In fact, Shanti had no serious interest in remarrying, and wasn't even inclined to have sexual affairs. She was more interested in capturing power in Bwana's household and acquiring as much financial muscle as possible. In money matters it would be hard to do better than Shanti in the acquisition and management of it. And in the process she would also be cutting her younger twin sister down to size.

One thing had emerged out of Shanti's stay in London. She became health-conscious. Her regular morning walk meant fast-paced rounds of the polo ground. She ate more fruit and less greasy stuff and heavy meals. All in all she managed to keep her slim figure and lively looks.

Nari wanted the arrangement to continue where Nargis would be with him for at least two weeks in a year—if Nargis was so willing. Nargis, of course, was ever willing. It meant some exciting days in London and a week or so at a Mediterranean resort—at times even a luxury cruise. And she came back loaded with purchases and presents. It's another matter that there was hardly anything for her mother.

Nargis showed keenness to meet her father every year. She liked his company and the way he looked after her.

19 Raminder's Side of the Story

I had a happy childhood. We lived in comfortable houses with large compounds and plenty of servants. My brother, older to me by four years, was always nice to me. Father, an officer in the Indian army, was often out on field duty. But when he was at home, the atmosphere was jolly. He joked and laughed a lot. And I was his favourite.

Mother was serious and a stickler for rules. She would insist on regular hours for homework after school, regular hours of sleep, and very limited TV watching. She was particularly strict about my movements, my associates, and ensured that I wore clothes that didn't show my body in any provocative manner.

By the time I was thirteen, father was posted as brigadier general at Jalandhar, the same post that Gen. Dwyer of Jalianwala Bagh massacre had once held. It was here that I learnt riding. I was athletic in school games, more so in running and jumping. We lived nearly four years in Jalandhar where I matriculated from a convent girl's high school in the first division. Brother was already in Khalsa College doing his graduation.

On more than one occasion, the doings of Gen. Dwyer came up for discussion. Father would agree that Dwyer was guilty of uncalled for brutality. Yet he had something to say in Dwyer's defence. Law and order had completely broken down in Amritsar. It needed strong action.

My father got promoted as a major general and was posted at the Army Headquarters, Delhi. I joined Lady Shri Ram College for B.Com. I was a day scholar and graduated in commerce.

In time, my father got promoted as lieutenant general and we moved our house from cantonment to Dupleix Road in New Delhi.

My brother had done his graduation but showed no real interest in studies. Father helped him to start a small hosiery mill at Ludhiana, which he did succeed in expanding and making good profits from it. Brother got married to a local girl.

It would be hard for people to believe but I had no love life till Udai, ADC to my father, began courting me. And at twenty, on my marriage day, I was a virgin. Within two years, Simran was born.

It was an idyllic life up-to the horrendous year of 1984.

That year, the army stormed the Golden Temple and Mrs. Indira Gandhi was shot down by her Sikh guards, something inexcusable, in fact despicable. It is a horrible crime to shoot someone whom it is your duty to guard. In retaliation, Hindu mobs started killing Sikhs in large numbers in Delhi and some other places. Udai had to rush up to Delhi to bring back my elder brother who had got trapped there on one of his business visits. As luck would have it, my father was on tour. I could never thank Udai enough for the rescue. In the same year, there was the Bhopal gas tragedy that killed thousands and maimed many more.

Then on the fateful 31st December of 1984 Udai died in a polo accident. Our loveable family friend and benefactor, Sarabjeet, got crippled in the same accident.

George Orwell's 1984 indeed turned out a most horrible year for me.

A year had passed since Udai's tragic death.

My life had been rendered lonely, difficult, often depressed. During the long hours when Simran was at school, it was hard to pass the time. I did nothing but daydream, dwell on memories, often biting my fingernails. It would be some years before I brought my nails back into shape so that I wasn't hiding my hands.

Then Father died suddenly of a heart attack one early morning. It left no time to call a doctor or move him to a hospital. I loved my father dearly and felt very sad over his passing.

Mother has been here for two months and might well be staying much longer. She would like to see me settled, preferably in Ludhiana.

Being of different generations, we had contrasting approaches to the business of living. Of course, she was some help in the kitchen and running of the house. Yet, usually, she created more problems than she solved. .Of late, arguments between us tended to become a bit acrimonious. Gurpal wanted me to shift to Ludhiana with my brother. She entertained the idea that I could marry someone there, preferably a Sikh gentleman of means. She was a tough little woman who always wanted to have her own way.

Gurpal frowned on my seeing Bwana too often. Indeed, it was not I visiting Devi House but Bwana visiting us. One day when Bwana left after longish stay, Mother said in exasperation, "Why does he come so often and stay so long?"

"He was Udai's best friend. He feels obliged to look after me. In fact, Udai's dying words were addressed to him, "Look after Rammi." And mind, a visit for him is no easy matter, handicapped as he is."

"Look after you, as a lover or as a brother! Better tie him a rakhi if it is such an innocent relationship."

I didn't respond, just kept mum.

My elder brother and his wife were here for a day. They made it out as a casual visit. But I was convinced that mother had called them to put pressure on me to move to Ludhiana. I liked my elder brother Surinder, a helpful, happy, friendly person. He has always been well disposed towards me. His wife was a dry, childless stick with a sharp tongue.

We kept sitting at the dinner table itself after the remains of an early evening meal have been cleared. Everyone was having tea while Surinder was nursing a brandy. Simran had her nightly glass of hot chocolate milk.

Addressing Surinder and his wife Harbans, the mother made out anew, "Now that you two are present, I'm again asking Rammi to move to Ludhiana. Anyway, how long can I stay on here?"

Harbans, well aware of my disinclination to quit Jaipur, piped in, "Mummy is right. What have we got here! Even the haveli belongs to Udai's family. They can reclaim it any day."

"Nobody has asked for it yet," I mumbled.

"The house in Ludhiana is huge. Rammi and Simran can have a separate portion," said Harbans, biting into a cookie. "And first-rate schools have come up in the city. My niece goes to one and is quite happy about it."

"Rammi, if she likes, can help in the management of the family factory; she has a degree in commerce. Here, she's left doing nothing the whole day except feeling bored," added Mother.

"All this is there," interposed Surinder. "However, Rammi has to decide for herself, not us."

"We can surely advise our daughter," cut in Mother. "Tell her what's good for her. To an extent she stays too shocked with Udai's sudden death to think coherently."

Simran, finishing her glass of milk and putting the mug down with a thud, shouted, "I'm not leaving my school. No Ludhiana for me."

"Don't shout, Simran. Speak respectfully," I told her curtly.

"But I'm not leaving my school, my city."

"You can't stay on if your mother goes," interrupted Harbans.

"I'll join the school hostel. Or, better put up with Uncle Bwana."

This made my mother, and even Harbans, raise their eyebrows.

"You mean, you'll prefer staying with someone you call "uncle" than staying with all of us," said Harbans sharply.

My brother tried to calm down things, "Simran had her say. We'll go with what Rammi decides. It's her happiness that's uppermost in our minds."

"Bhai ji, give me a year more to decide. I'd prefer Jaipur where I've been living since my marriage. But if I can't find any worthwhile activity or work to keep myself busy as well as earn something, then I can consider moving to Ludhiana. I'm really grateful to Harbans Bhabhi for her kind offer."

"The matter ends. We wait a year," said my brother, getting up after gulping his drink.

My mother, Harbans Bhabhi, and the elder brother were seen to be doing a lot of discussion regarding me. The three knew quite well that I won't be moving to Ludhiana, at least for a year or two. To them, a way out was to find someone suitable as a husband in Jaipur itself. It was then that my elder brother put forward the proposition that Balbir Singh, a Sikh contractor at Jaipur could be the best choice for the purpose. He had known Balbir since they were class-fellows at Khalsa College, Jalandhar. Balbir, thirty-seven, had stayed unmarried and had flourished in his business from contracts in making roads and buildings, particularly important government buildings.

Mother and Harbans were quite enthusiastic about it and persuaded my brother to see Balbir before leaving for Ludhiana. Surinder met Balbir, and the two were said to have a longish discussion on the subject. Balbir seemed to be excited about the proposal. He told my brother that he has seen me couple of times at Bwana's parties and was all admiration for my looks and behaviour. Indeed, he was so excited that he came along with Surinder to the haveli to meet Mother and Harbans, and possibly me.

I did show up for a few minutes but without any special dress and make-up.

Balbir appeared to be a handsome, muscular Sikh with brown penetrating eyes and a pleasing expression. He had tied his beard tightly with a string and was sporting a well-wound pink turban. He was a hairy fellow with the heavy eyebrows joined and luxuriant moustache. His hairiness could not be counted as a minus point as the woman proposed for marriage was herself a Sikh. He, however, had the uncanny tendency to bite the hair under his lower lip when feeling uncomfortable. Balbir appeared jovial and well mannered, somewhat more civilized than a normal image of a contractor who tends to be bossy because of daily dealings with labour.

Later, I overheard my mother telling Surinder and Harbans that she would pursue the matter of my match with Balbir. They seem to nod in agreement over this strategy.

"Sarabjeet is keen to have us for a meal before we leave," said Surinder. "I have accepted it but asked for an early lunch by twelve."

I could see Mother and Harbans going into a long huddle in the kitchen before dispersing. My brother talked to Simran about her school and studies while I tidied up the rooms.

Lunch at Bwana's went off well. Being Sunday, Kranti was home. She was all affability to Mother, my brother, and his wife. Her frosty looks she only reserved for me and Simran.

Bwana, she said, suffered severe back pain last night.

Yet he soon came down and was his usual genial, considerate host. He told us he was perfectly OK with a couple of painkiller pills.

Before departing, Surinder presented me with a heavy gold necklace. Simran got rupees 3000 to spend as she liked. And then they were off in their Toyota, leaving Mother behind with us.

Mother lost no time in pursuing her plan for me to wed Balbir. She would have long talks with him on the telephone. And then she began inviting him for tea and dinner at our place and would give extraordinary attention in preparing such meals.

Balbir turned out to be a well-mannered man, polite and courteous. And he never came empty handed. It would be a bunch of flowers, often another item such as a box of imported chocolates for Simran and a bottle of perfume for me. Even Mother would get something.

Despite a couple of visits and dinners, Simran never took a liking to him. She would just greet him and soon slip into her room.

Balbir was jolly company. He appeared well educated, well informed, and could look at the lighter side of things. We also learnt that he had by now a flourishing business. Four large buildings were under construction with him including a three-star hotel. He was also constructing a 10-mile stretch of a four-lane highway.

Balbir had his mother living with him. Only a month back she had gone to her younger son in Delhi whose wife was expecting a baby. To reciprocate our hospitality, he invited us for dinner at his place. Mother was enthusiastic in accepting it. I was non-committal while Simran frowned on it. Eventually, we all were driven to his place on the outskirts of the city. He lived in huge house with rooms well furnished and an extensive courtyard.

He offered mother and me a glass of wine while he had whisky with soda. Mother accepted the drink while I declined, despite his urging to have it.

At the dinner table, it was expensive china and silver cutlery. There were fish and chicken. And the whole meal topped by mouth-watering *kulfi*.

On the way home, Mother would say, "What a perfect host he is! Such good manners." And she added, "He must be quite rich. There was the bearer and a cook. Outside there was a guard and a driver of his Mercedes." Simran kept a sullen silence over Mother's litany of praise for Balbir, while I had to nod once or twice.

Within a month, Balbir arranged a day's picnic to the City Water Works situated on a hill top, some eight miles away. When he came around 11 to pick us up for the picnic, Mother feigned a headache; evidently she wanted me and Balbir to be the only two going for an outing. Simran excused herself saying she had a lot of school home work to do. I would have also liked to drop out but that would appear very unmannerly. So I agreed to accompany him. Got dressed into a pair of jeans and a white top. The Jaipur weather in September did not call for a jacket. Seeing me, Balbir exclaimed, "You are looking beautiful, with a figure slim and athletic." My response was a little smile, particularly when I had taken no pains for any elaborate dress-up.

He drove me in his Mercedes. Balbir knew of a place nicely sheltered among trees enjoying some privacy vis-à-vis other visitors. He had brought a nice carpet to be spread out, and quite a lot of food and drinks. He opened two bottles of ice cold beer and offered one to me.

I generally don't drink alcohol. Yet not to displease him I agreed to take a few sips from the frothy glass while he drank the rest of the two bottles. And he began looking at me with love in his eyes.

I opted for a light lunch of rice and meat curry followed by pieces of melon. Balbir appeared a hearty eater. He ate twice as much. After lunch, he suggested a short walk in the park. It was one of the most pleasant afternoons with a mild sun and a light breeze blowing. From the hilltop you got a great view of the sprawling Pink City. And down under was the huge lake shimmering in the sun. Balbir could not have wished for a more favourable setting to further his aim of seeking the lady's love. There he put his hand around my waist and was angling for an embrace. I released his hand and kept my distance.

"Are you allergic to me?"

"No, I like you. But we can only be friends."

"Why? I want to marry you."

"Any such marriage is out. I love someone else."

"You mean Sarabjeet? People talk of his nearness to you."

"You can put whatever interpretation you like. I can only be a friend with you and nothing more. So no physical advances, such as hugging or kissing."

"Alright. Let's be friends," he said in a despairing tone, though he kept holding my hand.

Indeed both of us knew that friendship of this type won't last long. He wanted sex and marriage, not mere friendship.

Mother must have learnt of the fiasco at the picnic from Balbir with whom she talked almost daily on phone. She seemed not to give up without making one more attempt. So she persuaded Balbir to come to a dinner at their place. This time Mother made full preparations for a grand dinner with the best of china and silver, and half a dozen savoury dishes. Balbir came dressed in a regular dinner suit with a fruit basket as a gift. In the drinks before the meal, Balbir was offered Black Label scotch and I was persuaded to have a small glass of French red wine. Mother had the same for herself.

Just as the meal was beginning, a door bell rang and rolled in Sarabjeet in his wheelchair. Mother was fairly ruffled to see him just at this time. I put on a welcome smile and had a place made for him at the table. Sarabjeet and Balbir knew each other and seemed quite friendly.

Sarabjeet said he couldn't stay for dinner as he has been invited to another one in the vicinity. He had just looked in before going to that place. And he wheeled out within minutes.

The elaborate candle-lit dinner again proved a flop. I absented myself from the dining table for nearly half the time. Simran, on her part, chose to eat in her own room.

By this time, both Mother and Balbir were reconciled to the situation that I was not willing to go into marriage with him.

In due course, Balbir's visits to our place became less frequent and eventually ceased.

Some years later, Balbir was reported to have married a woman from Amritsar. As far as I was concerned, I would wish him all the luck. He was a likeable person. Yet in my life nobody figured except Bwana.

I had no intention to marry anybody else. There was this army officer, a colleague of Udai, who started wooing me. He had sought premature retirement from the Cavalry Regiment and was running a successful breeding farm for riding horses. He had been widowed years back. Angad was persistent in his wooing. He kept on inviting me for dinners and outings which I politely declined on one pretext or the other.

"Why are you hesitant to come out with me," said Angad one

evening. "My intentions are honourable. I seek matrimony, not just a sexual affair."

"Angadji, I appreciate your sentiments. But I'm not going to marry anybody."

"Why? You look young and attractive."

"This is my final decision. There's going to be no marriage for me, to you or to anybody else."

"But we can be friends."

"Sure." Yet I knew fully well that Angad would soon discontinue coming, and this is what exactly happened. After a few courtesy visits, he never turned up.

Another colleague of Udai's, now commanding the Cavalry Regiment itself, was the other unwelcome visitor. He had a wife and three grown-up daughters but was looking for some easy sexual picking. I had to rebuff him rather rudely. It made me wonder why my husband's colleagues keep on making passes at me. They must be privy to the gossip of my intimacy with Bwana, even when Udai was alive.

20 Rammi's Business Venture

August 15, 1986. The day was Raminder's birthday, coinciding with India's Independence Day. Bwana was visiting her place in the morning, carrying a bunch of tulips and a Mikimoto pearl necklace.

He had come to greet Raminder on her birthday; he carried happy memories of her birthday celebrations in London where he kissed her for the first time, the only time. He knew that Raminder like being first on her birthday.

"Happy Birthday," he said, as he rolled his wheelchair into the haveli, helped by his driver. Giving him a nervous smile, she said, "I no longer have the heart to celebrate by birthday. Anyway, the pearl necklace would be too much for it."

Bwana consoled her. "The dead are dead," he said. "The living have to live their lives."

"I'm not sure whether I can manage any worthwhile thing in my life. At best, I look after Simran and limp along with my dull existence."

Then she brought him a slice of chocolate cake, along with a cup of coffee. "Simran," she said, "was keen about a cake for the occasion."

Rammi made out that her mother had left for Ludhiana last Sunday, with no indication as to when she would be back.

Sarabjeet could clearly notice that Rammi looked under the weather. She sat sad, listless. "Rammi, you can't brood the whole day. Must do something to divert your mind."

"I'm thinking the same. But what can I do? I've no experience in business. At best, I can teach in a school. Or give riding lessons to rich girls."

"But what would you like to do?"

"Don't know."

"Lately I've been giving some thought to it. What about running a beauty parlour? You know what women should do to look their best. Take some short training in Delhi. With summer vacation coming, Simran can go with you."

"Not sure whether I'm up to it. I have led too sheltered a life."

"I'm sure you'll do well. You are intelligent and you know how to handle people. Anyway, there's no harm in trying. I'll arrange for a beautician's training course. You stay at my place in Delhi."

And he continued, "The haveli you live in is not comfortable and is far away from Simran's school. Probably it will also be far away from your future place of work. I am thinking of building a block of three modern flats on the vaunted Sardar Patel Marg. A plot of 1000 square yards has already been acquired. My idea is to let you have the ground floor, Simran the first floor, and Nargis the top floor. What do you think of it?"

"That would be the most generous offer I could imagine."

"Good. The architect would come and see you for any suggestions you have. The place should be ready within a year for occupation."

Impulsively, Raminder stood up. Bending, she took his head in her hands and planted a kiss on each of his cheeks. He was a dear.

"Children are kissed on cheeks, not grown ups."

On this, Rammi gave a quick peck on his lower lip.

And she said, "But for you, I'd be nowhere."

"I'll always be by your side," Bwana said in his assuring tone.

By this time, Simran had stepped out of her room. Seeing Bwana she put up her arms around his neck and rubbed her head against his chest. There had developed a deep friendship between the two.

Learning of Bwana's scheme for the flats, Kranti did protest. "Papa, you are throwing away too much money on Rammi and Simran."

"Rammi is the widow of my best friend. Indeed, I do blame myself to some extent for the horrid accident that caused her husband's death and turned her into a widow. I must do everything possible to make her comfortable, if not happy."

Kranti knew that Rammi was not only the widow of Bwana's best buddy he was also in love with her since he saw her first. So she thought it better to keep quiet; she had some idea of the wrath of her father.

She, however, could not refrain from muttering that this gift will become a hot topic for silly gossip.

"Gossip there would be in any case," retorted Bwana.

Bwana arranged a three-month's short course in make-up and other beauty aids with a Delhi branch of L'Oreal. This proved really useful; Rammi was a fast learner in these matters. It also boosted her self-confidence. Simran, too, enjoyed her time in Delhi. She was fascinated with the sights of the city.

A year had gone by. Rammi opened a beauty parlour in Rambagh Palace Hotel, renting a couple of rooms in the commercial wing. Bwana did finance much of the equipment and furnishing. To Rammi's pleasant surprise, Kranti helped with her contacts in securing the premises, setting it up, and even getting some customers. Maybe, she wanted Rammi to strike an independent course than lean too heavily on her father. Who knows, with luck, Rammi may acquire a new lover.

The parlour was now paying itself, with a small margin of profit. There was a competent hairdresser and three girls for manicure, pedicure, waxing, and facial. During the marriage season they did many bridal make-ups, a lucrative part of beauty parlour business. The parlour in the hotel had also the advantage in attracting many female guests. As a policy, Rammi only entertained female customers. This would dampen any talk of sexual play there.

Rammi would be there by 11:00 a.m.—customers won't come before that—and stayed on till 7:00 in the evening. A packed lunch would come from Devi House, a few furlongs away. Often the food was so substantial she kept a part for the dinner. Simran mostly lingered at Bwana's place after school till they both went back home.

Raminder's work was relatively light: to order supplies in time, talk to customers, to keep the premises spotlessly clean, and supervise some make-up. In between, she read a lot on the subject of beauty care.

The work kept her gainfully busy. And, in the bargain, she was getting better at her own make-up, let alone the luxury of a captive hairdresser for hair washing and hair treatment, such as henna dyeing. All this brought back some of her former liveliness. She was more playful, smiled more and had resumed a regime of yoga.

The main factor in the success of the beauty parlour was the personality of Raminder itself; her pleasant talk with the customers, her graceful way of dealing with people and problems, let alone her charming manners.

By this time, they had moved to the new flats. What a change from the crowded city and the old-style haveli! Airy, bright, spacious rooms, modern kitchen, and bathrooms. There was the luxury of a lawn in front. And all this in a posh, open area of the city. Her residence was now nearer to the place of work and Devi House as well as Simran's school.

Simran occupied her first floor flat but kept eating down with her mother. She was now in college and wanted space and quiet for her studies. Shanti decided against renting the Nargis's portion; so it remained locked up.

Rammi mused, "I have to live my life here, educate Simran, and help her acquire a profession. She shouldn't find herself as helpless as I felt on Udai's death. In time, she will get a good match she can marry. She is growing into a pretty, smart girl who's fast shedding her uncouth ways and impulsive behaviour. She has grown into an attractive girl with deep dark eyes and long silken hair, a nice-looking nose, and inviting lips. Five feet six, she is developing pleasing curves at the chest and bum. Simran isn't choosy about clothes but is developing a personality hard to ignore. She has my dimples in her cheeks when she smiles. And on top of everything, she excels in studies. All in all, I have few worries on her score."

"With Udai gone, I lean on Bwana more and more. The love chemistry between us possibly waxed as strong as ever. At times, I experienced an almost uncontrollable urge to nestle into his arms, give myself to him. I love him for his own sake, not his money. And my love for him is no less because he has lost the use of his legs. I love Bwana as he is."

And Raminder's soliloquy continued.

"Are we destined to live apart when both of us could be pining for each other? Fear of scandal kept a curb on our frequent meetings, let alone the hawk-like watch over us by Kranti."

"How long will the suspense last! Can we defy public opinion in this conservative society to become a live-in couple? With Bwana's public image, this would be unacceptable. That leaves only the option of marriage if we had to secure our wished-for happiness. Seeking clandestine sexual encounters was no answer; indeed, it'd ruin the purity of our love."

"How our love life would fare in the coming years, I haven't a clue. But of one thing I'm well nigh certain; he's the only one I'll ever love, and in all probability he would feel the same for me."

21 An Extraordinary Offer

Simran was 23. She had graduated from Rajasthan University and then did a law degree. Raminder had favoured architecture or chartered accountancy.

"Mama, I want to be a lawyer. And I plan to practice in courts of law."

"The law practice is not ideally suited for women."

"My mind is made up. I want to be a lawyer."

This matter became the subject of discussion by the mother and the daughter with Bwana.

Let Simran do what she likes, was Bwana's studied response.

Simran was now a junior lawyer, working with a leading practitioner in the High Court, mostly at the Bench in Jaipur. Simran cut a dashing figure in the lawyer's black coat and was popular among her colleagues, even judges.

She lived in her own flat gifted by Bwana and drove her own car, a Maruti 800.

Often when Bwana and Raminder met in the evening, their talk veered to Simran's career and her possible marriage.

"Are you really anxious for Simran's early marriage? She is only twenty-three." Bwana had been asking.

"Yes, I'd feel relieved if she is nicely married and settled."

"For some time I'm having a suitable person in view."

"Who is the one?" she asked eagerly.

"Narinder Singh Ranawat. He is a member of the IAS and is presently working as Municipal Administrator of Jaipur City. I know the Rajput family, a noted one from Udaipur. My enquiry indicates that Narinder has a promising career and enjoys a good reputation, not someone like Nari."

"I think I have met him once or twice at your place. He is handsome and smart. I always found him well dressed. Displays pleasing manners."

"Good. I shall soon arrange that the two young people meet at dinner at my place. Let's hope they hit off. Subsequent negotiations you can leave to me."

The couple did meet at a select dinner at Bwana's place. They seem to like each other and did make a few car journeys to neighbouring spots. Narinder was keen on an early marriage; he was already nearing thirty.

Meanwhile, Bwana got in touch with Narinder's family to sort out the details of the proposed union.

Everything went off well, leading to an engagement. The marriage was to be solemnized in three months.

"Simran's marriage will take place from my house," declared Bwana, "and it will be a marriage as glittering as that of Shanti's."

Raminder hearing this, exclaimed, "I am overwhelmed by your generosity and help. Simran can't be having a better benefactor."

Kranti was in no way pleased with this development. It meant so much expense and dislocation, let alone people talking about the Bwana–Raminder relationship. She did mumble some objections. But Bwana overruled these.

"Simran has been like a daughter in this house. She will go out like one."

Kranti couldn't help mumbling, "This will look as if Raminder is your mistress."

Bwana gave a little laugh. "Well, I may be the mistress, not she."

Kranti deemed it better to slip away, though she'd concede some element of truth in Bwana's reply. After all, Raminder was the one pursuing, not so much he.

By this time Shanti and her daughter Nargis were back at Devi

House, probably for good. Shanti, though well disposed towards Raminder, was also not happy at so much money being spent on Simran's marriage. Indeed, this money could be better spent on the marriage of Nargis.

The marriage ceremonies were in full swing at Devi House. Tonight was the sangeet session, with the usual song, drinks, dinner, and subsequent dancing late into the night, with a DJ in attendance. The actual marriage ceremony was slated for the next day, a Saturday.

Like Shanti, Simran had also been gifted a car, a cream-coloured Honda City. The idea was that the married couple will drive out to their honeymoon at Shimla in the new car for a week's stay at the Cecil Oberoi.

By 10 p.m., Bwana, fatigued with the day's festivities and his troubled back, retired to his bedroom. He brushed his teeth, got into his bed clothes and crawled under the duvet.

While dancing was going on, Simran discovered that Bwana had retired to his bedroom. He had been her favourite uncle from childhood; in fact, the only uncle. As she grew up she would rush into his long arms and broad chest. Bwana would reward her with a peck on the cheek. She fully knew of the deep love between Bwana and her mother. Yet this didn't stop her from feeling a fascination for this wonderful man. And her heart would go out when she would see him in his crippled condition, a towering man laid low by a freak accident. She couldn't forget all he had done for her, and was doing still. This sent in her a wave of sympathy and love for him.

Unobtrusively, Simran slipped up to Bwana's bedroom. Soundlessly she entered. Seeing Bwana awake, she said, "With going into new relationships, I have come to bid you a private good-bye; a good-bye to one I hold most dear." She sat on his bed, pulled down the duvet, bent over him with her pointed breasts rubbing his broad chest, and she held his head in her hands. Then she began showering kisses on the forehead, eye-brows, cheeks and the unreceptive lips. Bwana did nothing but lock her in his long arms. Simran even dared run a hand on his stomach and down below. He did experience a mild tumescence but otherwise remained passive to her love ministration.

Indeed, Simran had a mind to gift her chastity—a one-time gift—to him, the only way she thought she could repay his generosity.

Bwana had a soft spot for this young beautiful girl. Yet he lay inert and didn't respond in any sexual manner to her kissing and rubbing. She gave him a final kiss and got up, saying, she will always have a special space in her heart for him. For the sex-starved Bwana, it called for a supreme restraint to deny himself a beautiful young body with her tantalizing offer of sex. Bwana was amazed at the girl's audacity, yet he couldn't help but appreciate her gesture, a highly pleasing one that he knew would always live with him as a happy memory.

Down she went and joined the dance party.

Raminder had noted her absence. On seeing Simran, Raminder enquired, "We were looking for you. Where were you?"

"I had gone up to bid good night to Uncle Bwana and did sit there for a brief chat."

Simran made up her mind that she would never mention the details of good-bye visit upstairs to her mother. This was a laudable silence as relationships between mother and a daughter can be very complex in such matters. And Simran was almost certain that Bwana would never divulge of the same to her mother or anybody else.

After marriage, Simran and her husband shifted to her flat above that of Raminder. She should be going to his work place while Simran would be busy with her court work. In time the couple was blessed with a baby boy, a beautiful chubby boy who rarely cried. As the baby grew up, Simran resumed her work at the court, leaving the baby in the care of the maid. Raminder coming back from her beauty parlour would often go up for the baby, now called Jogi, who would smile looking at her while she cuddled him. And soon he began to shout *nanni, nanni*, as he saw her. To Raminder, this was the most enjoyable hour or two of her day. Within two years, Simran and her husband moved to a government bungalow allotted to him on the known Hospital Road. Raminder would often drive to their house after her parlour's work to play with Jogi. And quite a few times they would send the boy to her place.

Part-III

22 The Wish-List

The twins knew that Bwana did not like any fuss on his birthday. Yet this was going to be no ordinary birthday; he would be fifty.

The twins planned for a cake and candles at the breakfast with the table decorated with flowers. Raminder and Simran were there having been alerted in advance. Simran also advised to bring her camera along. Nargis was to go up to her grandpa's room and bring him down. As Bwana came down and saw the decoated table with all the five female present, he exclaimed, "What's all this!" The twins shouted back, "Papa, you are fifty today. This calls for celebration." He countered, "I'm possibly too old for it."

"No, you are not," cut in Raminder. "The same youthful face without a single grey hair."

Bwana could just mutter, "Oh, my woes are only known to me."

Bwana was then asked to cut the cake and blow out the candles, while everyone sang "*Happy Birthday to You*". The big black-forest cake had 50 boldly engraved on it.

"Cheer up," said Simran, putting a piece of cake in his mouth, and kissing him on the cheek, and so did all around the table kissed his cheek.

Getting into a happy mood, Bwana said, "Each one of you can buy a present of your choice as a gift from me."

Bwana had invited Dr. Adoor for a quiet dinner that evening. After the meal, the two repaired to Bwana's office-cum-library. Adoor took out one of the Cuban cigars from his silver cascade on the centre table. Bwana helped light it with the shiny lighter while he nursed a cup of coffee.

"I'm not happy with my health," said Bwana.

"You are only fifty. What's the problem? You eat well. You sleep well. You have the right blood pressure. The back is troubled, but that is manageable."

"I feel a certain discomfort in the morning as I get up. Even find sweat on my forehead and chest. It looks as if a heart attack is coming. I understand most heart attacks occur in the morning hours when the body is getting ready for the day's activities."

"I don't think your discomfort stems from an impending heart attack. It could be from low blood-sugar level. Better eat a chocolate or two when you start sweating."

"Good. That's such an easy option. I'll try it out and let you know what happens."

The two friends sat silent for a few moments and then Bwana spoke, "I'm no longer sure of a long life. Something within me tells that my end may come sooner than expected."

"This may be a temporary phase through which you are passing. Perhaps it comes from your loneliness in bed."

"There's no early prospect of getting a bed mate. What about my writing a will!"

"There appears to be no immediate hurry for it, but you may well draw up a "Wish List" if you so desire. The actual will with the legal language can wait."

"Not a bad idea. Let me jot down a few points." And Bwana pulled out a note pad and unscrewed his pen, a silver Mont Blanc. He wrote itemwise, reading each one to Dr. Adoor.

1. The Devi House to remain undivided, along with its contents and cars, the property to be owned jointly by Shanti and Kranti.

   I have built Devi House into a beautiful dwelling place and it would be a pity breaking it into two. I know joint ownership by Shanti and Kranti will create its own problem, but I think they will be able to manage it; both of them love the house.

2. Shanti to get the London house.

   Shanti has lived in London and has links with it. If the London house is to be given to anyone, she is the best claimant for it.

3. Kranti to get the farm house and all that the farm contains.

   Kranti is capable administrator. She has already improved the farm, organized the staff and made it more profitable. She is well-qualified to run the farm.

4. Raminder to get the Golf Links Delhi house.

   As you know, Raminder is the widow of my best friend, my heart goes out to her, and I would like to provide some sure means of income to her. She can rent the Delhi house, or even sell it.

5. The city haveli to go back to my younger brother, and so also my share of ancestral land and properties.

6. Nargis and Simran to get one crore each from my liquid assets.

   The two are like daughters to me.

7. Shanti, Kranti and Raminder to get rupees two crore each.

8. All servants to get rupees one lakh each. Those with ten years service to get three lakh. Those with twenty years service to get five lakh.

9. The rest of my money to be made into a trust for building and operating a working women's hostel and aid to deserving girls in education.

10. Kranti will manage whatever is left of my business and would be entitled to its proceeds.

    As far as possible, she will give employment to my office staff.

11. My friend Dr. Adoor will be the sole executor of the Wish List.

"What do you say to that," asked Bwana.

"Not bad as a first attempt."

"Adoor, you keep this paper," Bwana said as he tore out the two pages from the note pad. "But this is only a Wish List. I have not even signed it. You have to prove my hand-writing if it came to that."

"You may have overlooked an important point," said Adoor, "What will happen if you and Raminder get married? The whole Wish List would call for a change, more so the disposal of Devi House."

Bwana remained silent for some moment and then responded, "I don't think it will be fair for me in this crippled state to ask for Raminder's hand. She deserves someone better. And in any case my twin daughters will kick up hell at the prospect of another claimant to Devi House and my other properties."

"Don't berate yourself like this. I have a haunch that some day you and Raminder will get married. Forget about the feelings of the twins. Anyway, they benefit quite well."

Bwana gave a little laugh. Meanwhile, Adoor folded the Wish List papers and put it in his jacket's breast pocket.

"I hope there'd be no need for these papers. You'll live many long years and write a legal will. Only I suggest that you keep the contents of that will secret. It leads to all sorts of trouble if the beneficiaries know what is coming to them. Very rarely everybody keep as it is satisfied. And in any case the will wouldn't come into operation during your lifetime."

The Wish List was supposed to be an exercise in loud thinking by Bwana about his assets. Yet, somehow Shanti had heard a rumour about some such document.

This impelled her to question her father about it. "Papa, you are said to have penned a Wish List of your assets. Is it correct?"

"How you came to know about it? It's only between me and Dr. Adoor."

"Papa, such things have the knack of getting known."

"Alright. I'll ask Dr. Adoor that you and Kranti should have a look at it."

"Thanks. That will be very nice. We are your daughters and the nearest ones to you."

A few days later, Dr. Adoor came with the Wish List. He had made a photocopy so that someone angry may not tear off the original. Bwana called both the girls to hear it.

With Bwana and the two sisters present, Dr. Adoor read out the contents.

Shanti shouted, "Papa, you have given Simran the same amount as Nargis. Nargis is your grand-daughter while Simran is only a friend's daughter. She is also married and settled in her profession."

"To me, both the girls are like my daughters and so treated equally."

"It's not fair," Shanti responded in dismay.

Then Kranti spoke out, "You have equated Raminder with us in the cash award of rupees two crore each. Do you think she is equal to us in your estimation? You have already gifted her two first-rate flats and now wish to give her the prized Delhi house. Papa, so much of gifting to her is unjust."

Bwana didn't respond.

There were few moments of eerie silence. Sensing that Bwana could explode in anger, Adoor spoke out, "Kranti, your protestations seem off the mark. What happens if Bwana married Raminder? The lady will get much more than what is there in the Wish List."

Bwana interjected, "In my disabled condition, I'm no match for Raminder. She deserved someone better."

Kranti cried out, "I'm sure Raminder will jump at your offer of marriage. Let's hope you don't make one."

"That's enough for today," said Bwana, and started wheeling his chair to the bar, signaling Adoor to join him.

23 A Union of Lovers

Raminder was the woman whom he had loved the moment he had set eyes on her, mused Bwana. Over the years he had lavished much affection and largesse on her and family members.

At forty-five, Raminder had retained an attractive form; athletic, slim and full of spirit. The skin was clear with no wrinkle showing. The eyes under those long lashes were sharp as ever.

She had been showing in no unclear terms her inclination to marry him, to live with him. Bwana was, however, uncertain whether he was any longer a fit person for her. He had no use of his legs and was not even sure whether he had retained his manliness. How could he foist himself on this loveable person with all his bodily failings? Losing the use of his legs had considerably diminished Bwana's will to live, even to enjoy life. His ever recurring mental tension could well lead to a stroke or heart attack.

There was a struggle rising in his mind as to whether he could take Raminder as his wife; someone who was running a successful beauty parlour and was being wooed by quite a few eligible men. Will it be fair to deny her a mate who can walk and dance, and who is sexually potent? Bwana had been thinking over this for years without coming to a definite decision. Balbir, for one, could have been clearly a better match for her.

Raminder was not unaware of the mental struggle agitating Bwana. She, in turn, was keen to encourage Bwana towards living a normal life. She also hoped that in time he may agree to marry her.

She would often tell him that she loved him for himself whether he can walk or not didn't make any difference to her love. She would go on to say that she would love to be his wife even if he has lost his manliness. He was the only man she would like to live with whatsoever his physical failings.

Raminder sometimes felt that she was born a naïve, not clever enough to get her way in life. Here she had been lying in bed alone for years and the man she loved slept alone a few furlongs away. Carried on like this, she would soon be a middle-age woman. Already she had begun dyeing her black silky hair to hide a grey one. Surely she should take more active steps to win her love and be Bwana's wife. She harboured a feeling that she had not been active enough in this pursuit. With Simran getting married, Raminder was finding herself living lonelier. Her day would pass in activities at the beauty parlour, but the evenings were getting hard to endure. She had taken to music in the shape of playing guitar. Another diversion was to take to reading novels, let alone the TV serials. The ideal of self-reliance kept eluding her. What she longed for was human company of a satisfying sort, not merely social gossip or playing cards. All in all she pined for Bwana's company and physical love.

A week had gone by since the Holi festivities. Spring was in the air with the Jaipur warm days and cool nights. Flowers were in full bloom, and her lawn was recovering its green.

Raminder invited Bwana to come for a dinner on a Saturday evening. She planned it to be a very special evening, an evening she hoped she would seduce Bwana into full sexual play. Whether she would succeed or not, only the evening will show.

Raminder busied herself for making every arrangement for his coming. This included having the pubic hair nicely trimmed and a leisurely tub bath in warm scented bubbles. The lush long hair had undergone a full treatment at the parlour during the day. A light facial makeup gave the final finish. The perfume chosen for the evening was Chanel No. 5, Bwana's favourite. She even took care to brush her teeth again.

For the evening, Raminder had chosen a cream-coloured chiffon blouse with a matching ankle-length skirt. And there was an absence of undergarments beneath the skirt. She didn't hamper herself with a saree or salwar-kameez. For the jewellery, she only wore the pearl earrings gifted by Bwana on her birthday—the day that had ended with their first kiss.

For the dinner, it would be grilled pomfret, boiled potatoes and beans, followed by strawberries mixed with whipped cream. She had taken care to prepare the meal herself. Geeta, the maid servant, had been given a day off.

Bwana came around 8:00 p.m. to her flat. After wheeling in, he told his driver Balwinder to take the Nissan back to Devi House. He would call for it. Evidently, Bwana tended to underplay his presence by not keeping his car there.

As Bwana settled himself on a sofa in the living room, Rammi brought in a bottle of scotch, two glasses and a jug of water.

"Macallan 25, the best single malt!" exclaimed Bwana. "That would be a treat. By the way, where did you get it from?"

"Udai had brought it on his London trip. The bottle remained unopened all these years."

"I'll help you to open it," said Bwana. By this time, Raminder placed a bowl of roasted cashew nuts before him.

Thereafter, she poured a generous portion in Bwana's glass and a smaller one in hers. They clanked glasses.

"It's so smooth," said Bwana taking a gulp. "I normally don't take whisky but this is very inviting."

Raminder nodded in agreement as she sipped hers.

"What about this bowl of roasted cashew nuts? You know I have a weakness for them," as he began munching a mouthful.

"Nuts can do no harm. Mahatama Gandhi is said to have been living mostly on nuts."

"I'm no Mahatama, and Gandhi wasn't drinking scotch."

"By the way, where is Geeta?"

"The maid's mother is seriously ill. I have given her a day off."

"Who's cooking the dinner?"

"Myself. And it will be a light one."

"Good. I need a light meal."

"You look a little restive, a little worried," remarked Raminder.

"Nothing in particular but the constant bickering between Shanti and Kranti does distress me. There is actually no reason for them to quarrel but they do all the time on matters big or small. Even the talk on the dining table is peppered with barbs, each one scoring points."

"Couldn't you do something to pacify their hostility?"

"Kranti had moved to the first floor bedroom to be near me. Shanti returning from London was not happy with this arrangement. She has to occupy the lower bedroom, her former place, with Nargis taking over Kranti's girlhood set of rooms. Shanti is all the time mumbling that she should be near to me as she was home most of the day while Kranti was often travelling out of Jaipur. Yet Kranti refuses to oblige, she likes the first floor bedroom, a much better bed suite. To Kranti, it seems to impart better status to occupy the bed suite near me."

"Shanti has a point. She is home the whole time and takes care of all the household chores," Rammi cut in.

"Evidently, Shanti wants to wrest as much power from her twin sister as possible. In fact, Shanti has no other interest but household matters—besides acquiring expensive jewellery and clothes. I have been asking her to take to golf. The game would occupy a few hours of her day. Bought her a new golf set, the high quality Japanese Honma. She did take half a dozen lessons from the club pro but has not been able to step over the initial threshold of golf. The result is she has given up the game, saying the play is so silly, chasing a white ball that refuses to go the way one wants it to. It seems she has no head for any serious, sustained activity requiring full attention and persistence. I have even tried to interest her in the use of a computer and did spare one of my staff members for teaching her computer use. In spite of all this, she is unable to send or receive e-mail messages. She remains virtually computer illiterate."

"As far as I can make out, in Shanti's opinion, Kranti should mainly concentrate on her travel agency, leaving the household management entirely to her."

Bwana knew that Raminder has a soft corner for Shanti, the two being on friendly terms.

"I am trying my best to be a peacemaker between the warring twins, but to no good result. I'm really at a loss what to do. A doctor friend told me that the twin coming later often tries to overtake the one that came out first. Perhaps this looks to be true. Kranti is taking the high horse when dealing with Shanti, to the resentment of the latter. The whole atmosphere of Devi House stands vitiated. Even the servants are taking sides. They get contrary orders from the two sisters on everyday matters."

"You need not disturb yourself unduly," rejoined Raminder. "In time the two sisters will find some way to live together and who knows one of the two may get married."

At this juncture, Raminder made up her mind to use the most crucial weapon in her armoury. She had already prepared herself for the evening, both bodily and mentally

"Now forget the hassles at Devi House for the time being. Relax and enjoy," urged Raminder. And she got up to refill his glass as well as hers, his double in quantity to that of hers.

Bwana, a moderate drinker, was compelled to say, "Aren't we drinking too much?"

"This is going to be a special evening. You better say good-bye to your inhibitions." And saying this she sat in his lap and gave him a long loving kiss."

Her gesture sent a thrill into Bwana's body. Bwana in a loving mood, exclaimed, "Rammi, there is no one for me other than you."

"Then marry me," she shot back.

Bwana was almost stunned at this sudden direct approach. He didn't imagine Raminder being so forthright. He couldn't help asking, "Are you sure of what you're saying? Or is it under the influence of whisky? Have you thought of it that I'm a cripple and even my manliness is in doubt?"

He carried an impression that Raminder would not hesitate to marry him, but was it fair to her to be burdened with a cripple. That would be a very unfair deal for the lovely lady who he knew was being wooed by several suitors, all of them physically fit. So Bwana exclaimed after a moment's pause, "Many thanks for your offer and the way you elevate me. Yet give this matter a good deal of thought. Don't decide on sentiment itself."

"Dear Bwana, I have thought over this a lot during all these years. You are the only one I love and the only one I will marry if at all. Balbir and others have no fascination for me." And she continued, "Long years have gone by with me waiting for a union with you. These have been lonely years, with me sliding from youth into near middle age. How long you'd like me to wait?"

"I have loved you as I loved nobody else. But with my legs gone, I'm no longer a fit match for you. Rammi, you better marry Balbir or someone like him. You are one of the lucky women who improve with age. You would even be attractive at seventy."

"Thanks for the compliment. Attractive or not, I'm only for you and no one else. By the way, a famous American president, I think Roosevelt, married in a wheelchair, his legs stricken by polio."

"But I'm no Roosevelt … and I was told he was sexually potent."

"Sex, I suppose, is more to do with the mind than with the body."

Bwana's reaction was a few moments of silence.

"We could even live together without marriage. I understand that live-in couples are getting more and more common in many parts of the world. It seems that this set-up is gaining more social acceptance." said Raminder.

"Already we are a top subject of city's gossip. Living together will blow into a major scandal, more so in my social position. On top, the twins will kick up hell over any such arrangement. Rammi, think over the matter coolly. I am perhaps fated to live a lonely life. In any case, there would be never in my life or thoughts any one but you."

"Forget your physical problems. They don't matter to me at all. I can marry you tomorrow. Possibly, we could both go to London coming summer. Marry in a temple there or in a court of law. Live a few months in London and then come home married. All the gossip will die down."

"Rammi, don't be sentimental and decide straightaway. Take your own time … say six months. It's too important a decision for you to make in a hurry."

"My mind is made up, but as you say, we can wait for some more time. By the way finish your drink," she said, and gulped down her own. Adroitly she steered Bwana into her adjoining bedroom, an attractively furnished place. The lighting stood subdued.

She made Bwana lie back on the broad springy bed. Raminder began taking off her clothes one by one; the blouse, the bra, and finally the skirt. And there she stood before him all nude.

To Bwana, watching her shedding of each garment was a revelation;

his lifelong dream to see her naked body, such a tantalizing body. There were the mid-sized breasts that stood firm and inviting. He had seen these globes for years but hidden under clothes. This was his first glimpse of these being nude and he was rapturous about it.

Then his eyes strayed down to the smooth stomach, narrow waist and then the nicely-trimmed hair in the pelvic.

And in this inviting condition, Rammi unbuttoned his shirt to reveal the broad hairy chest. Soon thereafter, she pulled off his trousers and the Jockey shorts. His legs had thinned but not to an alarming degree.

Rammi leaned on his chest, took his head in her hands and kissed him on his forehead, cheek, and lips. In frenzy, she even tugged at his thick hair, her own long ones falling over Bwana's body. Thereafter, she slid a hand on his stomach and down below. Bwana could only reciprocate by kneading her inviting breasts, gently rubbing her stiffened brown nipples between his thumb and forefinger, and then enveloping her in his long arms.

Rammi was now using all the tricks known to her to arouse Bwana. She could already sense a certain tumescence coming on. She worked on it with her hands, even lips, and was gratified to find it taking a hard, formidable form.

At this point, she eased herself gently on it and began moving up and down; she was a rider. Bwana on his part kept on grasping her comely breasts with his two hands. And then he exploded with a mighty groan, followed by a shiver, Rammi not far behind in her coming with moans. It was Bwana's first ejaculation after the polo accident, a lapse of almost fifteen years. Again, it was Rammi's first sexual experience for all those years. The two lay side by side in a relaxed loving mood. To Bwana, it afforded a tremendous mental and physical relief. He was at least a man, even if crippled. He would recollect the words the doctor at the rehab centre said to him while leaving, "You will require a loving woman who would patiently and endearingly invoke your sexual rejuvenation". The words of the doctor had come true.

To Rammi, it also signified much relief, not so much for her sake but for the mental peace of Bwana.

Washed, dressed up, the two were at the dining table for a light meal of grilled pomfret, potatoes and beans (heated in the microwave), followed by strawberries in cream. It was agreed that on the first of the next month (two weeks away), they would travel to London and get married there in a temple or in a court of law.

Bwana and Raminder were preparing for the projected London trip in relative secrecy. They knew that any talk of their travelling out together would trigger another avalanche of gossip. Packing was minimal as he did keep clothes and other necessities at his London house. Rammi was advised to pack little; her requirements could easily be bought in London.

The news that Bwana was going to London with Raminder was not broken by any of the two, yet it did leak out through members of the staff who were making arrangements of air tickets, visas and travel health insurance.

"Papa, I understand Raminder is going to London with you," spoke out Kranti at the breakfast table.

"Yes, that's correct. She wanted a holiday and I offered to take her along."

"The two of you alone in the London house; this may lead to some unexpected development."

"Whenever two human beings interact there could be developments," cut in Bwana.

"Raminder may use this opportunity to pressurize you into marriage."

"She could pressurize me here itself. She doesn't have to go to London for it."

"Papa, do you realize that the local gossip mills will go into overdrive when they learn of you two going to London?"

"I don't care. We have been a subject of gossip for umpteen years."

Shanti who had kept silent until now and who was well disposed towards Raminder, was also alarmed at the prospect of another woman living in Devi House and claiming part of Bwana's inheritance.

"Papa, be a little more explicit about your plans. You have to confide in us. We are your daughters, the ones nearest to you," said Shanti.

"There is nothing to explain. It's my usual London trip every summer. If you want to come along, you are welcome, too."

Raminder encountered a somewhat similar probe. Her preparations for travel, especially arrangements for running the beauty parlour during her absence didn't escape Simran's notice. Raminder had planned that in her absence, Mona, the Nepalese hair dresser, would be in charge of the beauty parlour. This lady was known to be honest in money dealings and could keep control over the staff. Simran would be asked to visit the parlour once a week, see the accounts, order supplies, and to look into any other problems.

"Mama, why are you going to London?"

"Just on a holiday for a month or so."

"Are you going with Uncle Bwana?"

"Yes, we are going together."

"Mama, do you expect anything special on this trip?" Simran would have welcomed a marriage between her mother and Bwana but she wasn't the inquisitive, investigative type. And so she didn't pursue this matter of marriage.

Raminder told Simran to make a weekly visit to the beauty parlour and inspect things. At one time, Raminder thought she could ask Shanti to take over, but then realized Shanti was not up to hard, sustained work. Anyway, Shanti was too busy with her rummy sessions, shopping, and social engagements, besides looking after Devi House and Nargis.

The forthcoming London trip and the anticipation of imminent marriage got Raminder into a glow of love and pleasure. Her life would soon be full of fun and joy.

24 A Twist to the London Trip

Within a week to go for the London trip, another tragedy struck Bwana. He slipped in his bathroom, possibly over a patch of soapy water on the marble flooring and broke his right arm at the wrist.

Normally, Bwana took his daily bath helped by Hari, the valet. As luck would have it, on that particular morning Hari was running high temperature and shivering feverishly. Ordinarily, Hari would come on his bathing duty even when not feeling well, but this morning he just couldn't get up from his bed. Bwana was not inclined to call any other servant as he had to be nude in the bathroom. Hari was the only man who helped him bathe. So this morning, as Bwana climbed out of the high tub to wriggle his way to the bed, he slipped on a patch of soapy water and landed on his right arm. A sharp pain shot in his wrist. He hoped the pain would go away. Finally, he scrambled to his bed, dried himself, and with some difficulty got into his clothes. The pain in his wrist was escalating by the minute. So at breakfast he rang up Dr. Adoor to come and see him. Dr. Adoor who was very busy at that time came by eleven. Meanwhile, he advised Bwana to pop in a painkiller. On arriving at Devi House, he felt Bwana's wrist, which had swollen by now.

"I think you might have broken a bone," he said. "You have to come with me to the hospital for an X-ray as well as for examination by an orthopaedic colleague of mine."

"It can't be as serious as that," mumbled Bwana. "Pity, I didn't skip bath today in the absence of Hari. And between us, this injury has come at a very inopportune time."

The X-ray of Bwana's wrist showed a major fracture.

"I'm afraid it's a bit of bad luck for you, said the orthopaedic surgeon. "The wrist bone lies fractured, and for a right-handed man like you it will entail much hardship till the bone joins."

"That's correct," admitted Bwana, "I mostly use my right hand for everyday activities."

Bwana's wrist was set back and covered with plaster. With the wrist not bending, his right arm lay rendered virtually useless, more so with the legs being paralyzed.

"How much time it will take for the wrist injury to heal?" queried Bwana in dismay.

"You have a complicated injury at a crucial spot. It should take around two months for you to put your right arm into full use."

Bwana is back at Devi House. Adoor said, "He will come in the evening and they can discuss his future plans."

Shanti and Kranti made a lot of fuss over their dad's injury. They were full of expressions of sympathy and vowed to help him in day-to-day activities. Of course, for shaving he will have to get a barber. Hari came up for work the next day despite his fever; his master's welfare was too important to him.

In a way, Kranti was not unhappy over the development as it would delay her dad's departure to London in company with Raminder. Who knew anything could happen during the coming two-three months? She will in any case try to torpedo the move of the couple to London. Shanti was more concerned with her dad's injury and mental tension. Yet she was also not enamoured at the prospect of Raminder coming in as the lady of the house.

For Raminder it was a bombshell. She deemed herself unlucky in her plan for happiness. Was she a sort of curse on whom she lavished love? Udai died in a polo accident before her eyes. Her life's love stood crippled. Now when she was on the verge of marrying Bwana, he had suffered a nasty fall that broke his wrist. Surely, they couldn't go to London for two-three months, if not more. Who knew what would transpire during this period? The twin daughters could pressurise him to abandon his plan for marriage to her.

With right wrist in plaster, Bwana was finding it difficult even to leave Devi House, and so his visits to her place became rare. Raminder would, of course, come and see him once or twice a week, but then she often met the hostile glances of Kranti. Even Shanti, she sensed, had begun avoiding her.

Once when she met Bwana, tears came into her eyes and trickled down her cheeks.

"Why tears, my dear?" queried Bwana. "Everything will go alright."

"I don't know. I may be under some curse. Whomsoever I love gets into trouble. Udai died, you became a cripple, and now when our plan for marrying was maturing, there comes this debilitating injury."

"There's nothing like that. Cheer up. Give me your dimpled smile. As long as there's life in me you should have no worry."

In a gush, Raminder rose up and planted a kiss on his lips.

Raminder's misgivings were allayed to some extent when Bwana told her in private that his mind was made up to marry her. At worst if he can't go to London, he would marry her here in Jaipur or some other city in the country. She had just to be patient for a few months.

The orthopaedic surgeon had the plaster taken off within one and a half month and declared that the bone had healed well. Bwana could get back the full use of his hand within another month or so, duly helped by physiotherapy.

As soon as the wrist was near the normal, Bwana renewed his plan for London trip along with Raminder. As expected, there were some hostile looks from Kranti and even Shanti. Bwana, however, chose to ignore their unspoken protest.

25 The Longish Honeymoon

The two marriage hopefuls flew to London. Both were bubbling with excitement and joy. This was going to be a culmination of their deep sex-starved love spanning over some twenty-five years. With Udai's demise, Bwana was the only man in Raminder's affection. She had pined for the day when she could be one with him, her lover, her benefactor, indeed her main support in life. To Bwana, there could be nothing more pleasing than to live with Raminder as husband and wife. Her company had become all the more precious to him in his crippled condition. She was the one who could revive in him happiness and the joy of living. Indeed, there union will be the most fitting finale to their unusual yet unrivalled saga of love.

Settling in their London house, Raminder procured a bridal dress. Bwana wore a silk achkan, with a pugree to match. The two in their marriage gear got themselves photographed by a professional. Bwana kept a serious face, but Raminder was all smiles. The two arranged to have their marriage solemnized in a prominent Hindu temple, two of Bwana's friends acting as witnesses. Thereafter, they got the marriage registered in a court of law.

To Bwana's surprise and amazement, Raminder at forty-five was as ravishing as she was at twenty-five. She seemed to have the same slim body and the same nimbleness of limbs. Indeed, she appeared more appealing than ever before.

Rammi revelled in sex-play. To her surprise, Bwana was reciprocating in full measure, as if years of sex-starvation had stored up all those missed ejaculation. She was brimming with self-confidence, looking forward to a life of love and happiness. This time, she had the advantage of looking after Bwana in his day-to-day functioning, even giving him a morning bath, taking him around, and otherwise being useful to him in numerous other ways. All this yielded her immense satisfaction, made her love Bwana more and more.

In turn, this was producing a spark in Bwana's life and future full of happiness, almost overcoming the tragedy of his physical disability.

Bwana and Rammi decided that they would stay on in London for a year or so. They were keen to enjoy each other's company—had waited for it for years—with no other family member present.

The two also discovered that it was much easier to operate in London in a wheelchair than in Jaipur. Here the street pavements were smooth enough for his wheelchair, both the motorized and the other one. You could roll into restaurants, theatres, big stores, museums, and most of other places. Indeed, he saw quite a few others moving in wheelchairs. It seemed that in the advanced world, far more disabled people were mobile than back home. This was in complete contrast to places like Jaipur where the uneven pavements made the use of wheelchair almost impossible. Again, pavements in Jaipur were often taken over by vendors, hawkers and beggers. And the people walking looked at a wheelchair as an oddity, some as a curiosity. In London people seem to be socially tuned to facilitate the passage of wheelchair users and other disabled without embarrassing them with any special notice. "So many people in wheelchairs!" exclaimed Raminder.

"People lost legs in wars, car crashes and other accidents. Yet these people are keen to live a normal life. In our country the disabled mostly lead restricted lives, staying at home."

"I'm sure you will remain mobile when we go back."

Bwana smiled in affirmation.

They had worked out a daily routine. After breakfast, Bwana would spend an hour telephoning to his office over business matters. It was also meant talking to Kranti and Shanti, and often with Dr. Adoor. Rammi in turn would ring up her assistant at the beauty parlour and so also Simran. This morning hour was best for telephoning to India as it would be afternoon there. Sometimes, persons at home and office wanted Bwana back for sorting out various problems. Bwana, however, didn't plan to go back unless there was an emergency. Kranti, he was confident, could handle most of the situations aptly.

Raminder would then wheel him to a health centre, some two furlongs away. Here Bwana underwent an hour of physiotherapy, did some yoga exercises, and then took a longish swim in the pool. They usually ate at a nearby Italian restaurant.

Returning home, it was a midday nap, often accompanied with love play. At time when his mood dictated, Bwana would slide his strong right arm under Raminder lying by the side and pull her up over his body. Raminder usually wore a housecoat that opened up wide with a tug. Yet she had to undo half a dozen buttons of his shirt. "Wish," she said, "your shirt had a zipper which I could just pull down." Raminder took delight in pressing her naked breast against Bwana's broad hairy chest, her face on his face, and her hair falling on one of his shoulders. The move often culminated in sex-play. Both of them being sex-starved for years, the two seemed bent on making it up for the lost time. Raminder was the one who mostly indulged in love-play while Bwana lay on his back.

In the evening, they would have a drink and eat a light meal, see TV, or listen to music. Or, go out to see a film or a play preceded by supper there, mostly of fish and chips. On some days they travelled to watch polo matches or be at the races. One popular outing for them was high tea at Ritz, with cucumber sandwiches and Darjeeling tea. The Ritz also brought them memories of their dinner on her birthday and the subsequent first kiss. Another popular outing was to Hyde Park, with tea and cake in a restaurant near the Serpentine.

Raminder acquired a fair amount of high quality lingerie. To her wardrobe, she added a fur coat with a matching fur cap and snow boots. In fact, she liked the cold of London and would take walks regularly.

Raminder also took an opportunity to visit a few reputed beauty parlours. Here, she would have her own hair treatment, facials, pedicure, and manicure. In the process she learnt many new methods of beauty treatment. And she succeded in making some valuable contacts that would render advice and supplies to her beauty parlour in Jaipur.

Bwana, in contrast, didn't add anything to his wardrobe except a jacket of Harris tweed, the premier British tweed known for its coziness and durability.

During January and February when London was at its coldest, they moved to a hotel cottage in Cyprus. It was fun going around in the island and enjoying Mediterranean weather and cuisine.

This was the near blissful existence that the two had envisaged. After years of separation and loving they were together, undisturbed by others.

To the two, it was a culmination of their saga of love for some twenty-five years. You could notice a special shine on their faces and a certain sparkle in their eyes. Who knew about the future but the present could not have been happier than this.

26 The Knives Are Out

How were things going on in Devi House during the long, indefinite absence of Bwana?

Matters began rather smoothly between the twins. The two agreed that Shanti will order the everyday purchases for running the household, keep accounts, and pay the staff.

The amity didn't last for long beyond one month of Bwana's absence. On being recalled from New York, Kranti had occupied the first floor bedroom suite to be near Bwana in his own first floor suite. Shanti, on reverting from London, was keen to occupy the upper room which was not only more comfortable but also more prestigious. "I'm home all the day while you are out on your work and travels. It'll help if I'm close to Dad's room," she argued with Kranti.

Kranti shot back, "Dad is staying in London. Don't know when he will be back. And mind, when they return, Raminder as the wife will take over this room. It is futile for us two to fight over it." And Kranti continued, "You should actually be near Nargis and Nargis is putting up on the ground floor."

Thereafter a dispute arose about the use of the library-cum-office room, the best room in the house. Shanti wanted to share the room. She said that I have accounts to prepare, cheques to issue, and keep receipts. I need an office. Kranti retorted that you could very well use the table in the side room for this work.

"But why can't we share the main office? There is enough space for the two of us."

"I'm to perform all the office work pertaining to Dad's business. I have to meet callers for the purpose and keep confidential papers. I don't think it will be advisable to share the room. Anyway, it is basically a library and you have no interest in books."

Shanti had really no reply to this oblique sarcasm of her well-read sister.

And there the matter ended, at least for the time being.

Now the first blood had been drawn. It would be a matter of time before somebody made the next one-up move.

For some time, Jacob had been finding it problematic to secure an unoccupied hotel room for love making with Kranti. At time, all the rooms in the hotel were booked. And he got hints that the management disapproved of his practice, as it could lower the hotel's image.

Kranti came up with a quick solution. Why not meet in her house? To her, the most comfortable place for love making would be her own bed in the well-appointed suite. So it came down to Jacob coming to Devi House once a week for dinner and later the couple would slip into her suite. The guards often saw Jacob leaving in the early morning hours.

Soon this arrangement came to be known by the whole household-guards, drivers, cooks and bearers, not to mention Shanti herself. To Shanti, this was scandalous, something intolerable. And she lost no time in accosting Kranti about it.

"Jacob is here with you on some nights. Dad would have never allowed such a thing. It's a shame for Devi House. You will have to stop this practice."

"This is not something to be so worked-up about," responded Kranti. "Anyway, this is my bedroom and I'd do what I like there."

"I won't allow it," shrieked Shanti. "If you don't stop, I'll tell Jacob to get out. The reputation of Devi House is very dear to me."

"It's alright. Cool down. I'll work out something else."

Kranti, realizing that she was on slippery ground, had to concede defeat. She planned to have such nights with Jacob at the farm house with fewer prying eyes.

Yet she couldn't help shouting back, "You get half a dozen women for rummy for the whole afternoon and evening. Such a noisy lot! And a couple of naughty kids coming with them. These kids run amok all over the place. One urchin has broken a Venetian cut glass vase. Another was merrily throwing all sorts of things into the swimming pool."

"We are just having a harmless game of rummy," insisted Shanti.

"I don't know about harmless. But these ladies consume maunds of sweets and dried fruit. Why can't other participants take turns arranging rummy at their houses?"

"It's my house and I can invite whom I like," retorted Shanti. "You invite so many travel agents and even travellers to cocktails, and I don't say a word."

The spat between the two sisters ended in further acrimony. It seemed that living under one roof for the twins was getting more complicated than it looked. In fact, they couldn't stand each other for any length of time.

Shanti would recall nostalgically how they had been so close during their girlhood. Kranti would defend her against bullies, and Shanti would keep secret any wrongs done by Kranti. The two had grown up bonded by love. By this time, the knives were out.

The two sisters continued to live in Devi House despite their bickering and differences. Shanti was spending her time doing shopping, attending lunches and dinners, playing rummy, frequenting a beauty parlour, gossiping with a couple of former confidents and keeping an eye on Nargis. She didn't want to go to Raminder's beauty parlour because the staff there wouldn't have accepted money from her, and getting free service would prove embarrassing after a few visits. The management of the house itself took an hour or two of her time.

Kranti on the other hand, left for office in the morning and was normally back late in the evening. She not only managed her travel work but also sorted out various problems of Bwana's business. She caught an accountant in his office who was fudging with figures and siphoning out money. She affected much economy in the running of the farm, such as selling away polo ponies, converting the farm house into a luxury guesthouse, and later parceling out parts of the farm to builders for apartments. And for all this she did obtain her dad's prior approval. She even managed a land deal in Kota town that was proving profitable. All in all she was showing a flair for business competence and work management.

Only late in the evening, she would disappear for a dinner party and lively male company. By this time, the Jacob affair was mostly off and she had yet to acquire a steady sexual partner.

The same sex twins, they say, often develop jealousy for each other when they grow up. It is generally the later-born who become jealous of the first-born about leadership and parental love. The equation between our twins was turning out different. Shanti the first-born was getting jealous of the second-born; jealous of Kranti about her competence in business and managerial talent. On her part, Kranti was developing something like contempt for her less read, inadequate first-born.

One day, Shanti returning from a rummy session that extended late into the evening, found Nargis missing. "Where's Nargis?" she enquired from Hari.

"She has gone with Kranti Bibi to a dinner party."

Shanti was not happy about it. She knew her sister's sluttish ways and feared that Nargis could indulge in something similarly foolish. Shanti waited and waited anxiously. All her efforts to contact her sister on her cell phone failed because Kranti had switched off her phone. There and then she decided that she'd get the 16-year-old Nargis a cell phone.

Kranti and Nargis came in around 1 a.m. in high spirits. With Kranti going up straight to her bedroom, Shanti accosted Nargis, "Where have you been? It's past midnight."

"We went to a bonfire party held for an American tourist group of Kranti aunty's. It was at the Oberoi. There were drinks, dancing, dinner with a roaring fire in the middle. Great fun it was."

"In the future, you realize you'll have to take my permission before you go out with Kranti to such parties."

"Mama, it was such fun I enjoyed every moment of it."

"Did you drink?"

"Just a glass of red wine, my first drink. It wasn't bad."

"You aren't allowed to take a drink till you are eighteen, and in no case with male strangers."

"Kranti aunty was with me."

"Did you dance with any man?"

"Only with two young Americans, lads of eighteen to twenty. One fellow taught me how to dance the waltz."

"I just don't like it," said Shanti and marched up to her bedroom.

Next morning at breakfast, she broached the subject with her sister.

"Kranti, please don't take Nargis on your wild parties."

"Last evening, it was just fun. No vulgarity about it."

"You know what you did at fourteen. I don't want Nargis to follow in your footsteps."

Soon, even the breakfast discussion ceased. Kranti would get breakfast in her room and push off to work. They were twins, but by now it could be seen that there could be no two individuals more different in nature and more intolerant of each other's company than Shanti and Kranti.

To the outside world, Devi House seemed to run rather harmoniously. The elaborate Diwali and Holi functions were celebrated with the same gusto, though some spirit in these was missing in the absence of Bwana.

Our warring twins had their bickering everyday over one thing or the other. It often made both of them wonder as to how long they will manage to stay under one roof. Evidently, they would have to go their separate ways sooner or later.

27 A Matrimonial Fiasco

Shanti wasn't the one to go in for sexual affairs. A cousin of Bwana's wanting to make passes at her was rebuffed. She was quite reconciled to the existing state of separation with Dr. Nari. The separation grant sent annually by Nari would be there for another five years and that was a lot of money. So it was no surprise that she cold-shouldered a couple of suitors who were keen to marry her, more for her property than herself.

Things, however, were taking a novel turn. A leading businessman had come into the picture. Ajit Singh Rana was a prominent landlord. He also had a factory in Jaipur making plastic buckets, pans and mugs. Being flushed with funds, he was playing the market, dealing with stocks and shares. Bwana knew him well. And they had come closer when Bwana also started investing his money in stocks and shares. The two would meet once a month or so and discuss the market trends.

Rana, a forty-year-old Rajput, was five feet ten inches tall with a fair complexion, and light brown eyes. The most distinguishing feature of his face was the neatly trimmed moustache, half an inch of bushy growth well-tended. He had an athletic body being a regular tennis player, and a thick crop of hair on his head, all black with no grey showing. Rana was always seen dressed in smart western clothes. The only visible flaw in his looks was a stubby chin and a short neck.

Three years back, Rana and his wife were involved in a serious car accident. On a return trip from Delhi to Jaipur, a truck coming from the opposite lane had lost control, crashed through the divider, and hit their car. Rana in the driving seat escaped with minor injuries but his wife sitting in front was hit on the head with a metal piece and failed to survive. The couple had remained childless.

Rana's visits to Devi House continued after Bwana's departure to London. Rana seemed to have set his eyes on marrying Shanti. He would visit every Saturday by tea time, knowing that Shanti didn't have a rummy session on Saturday. He'd always come bringing a bunch of flowers and a packet of high quality chocolates, and sometimes a bottle of Opium, a favourite with Shanti. Again, he would bring something for Nargis, a book or a pen. He would sit there regaling Shanti and Nargis with his witty talk—he was a product of Mayo College, Ajmer, and St. Stephen's, Delhi. During these visits, he also came in contact with Kranti who would bandy jokes with him. You could well say that he was all courtesy and good manners. His invitation to Shanti for a dinner out had not yet been accepted. However, he had become a welcome figure at Devi House.

For the first time, Shanti began to entertain the idea of remarriage. After all, she was only thirty-seven with a beautiful face and an attractive body. She took care of her makeup and wore choice clothes. Lately she had also taken to yoga, devoting an hour to it in the morning.

Rana was all that one could expect of a suitor. He was fairly young, widowed without children, rich, handsome, with captivating manners. He lived in a grand house on the premier University Road. And as far as she could learn, his personal life was not blemished by sexual scandals.

Shanti was set against any love play before marriage. What she was aiming for was an improvement in social relation with Rana to the point that might lead to an actual marriage.

Things between Shanti and Rana were proceeding rather smoothly till one evening when a catastrophe struck.

Rana as usual had come on Saturday by 4:30 p.m. To his dismay, Shanti hadn't turned up from the beauty parlour. He learnt that Shanti was due to attend a marriage dinner party and so was taking extra care about her hair and make-up. There was a message that she'll be back by 5:30 p.m. as the parlour was too crowded.

Meantime, Kranti had breezed in after a game of tennis at a nearby club. She was alluringly dressed in a hip-high skirt and a top that showed a good deal of cleavage. After some genial talk with Rana she moved into the office-cum-library. A little later, she called him in. Rana was happy to oblige as he was getting bored sitting alone.

How it all happened was not clear to him later. But soon they were embracing and kissing. And then Kranti was bending over the big writing table with her drawers on the ground and Rana making thrusts from the back with his trousers round his ankles. And as he was climaxing into her, the door suddenly flew open, with Nargis romping in. Pity, they had missed bolting it. Nargis had returned from school and was excited to tell aunt Kranti that in the school play, *The Merchant of Venice,* she had been given the major role of Portia. The teenager was shocked to see what was happening. She beat a hasty retreat and plumbed herself belly-wise on her bed, completely distraught and confused, her head whirling over what to do next.

The two actors had seen the girl looking at them in amazement. Both were stunned in their own way with the unexpected escalation of an unplanned encounter into, quite likely, a harmful scandal.

Rana wound up and went home. Kranti resumed her work in the office after using the adjoining washroom.

Shanti came home around 5:30 p.m. and was dismayed to find that Rana had not waited for her. And he had also not left any message as to why he had to leave.

Going into Nargis's room, she saw the girl lying prostrate on her bed, showing no interest in acknowledging her mother's presence.

She nudged Nargis to get up.

"What's wrong? Has anything happened at school?" Nargis didn't respond.

"Come on tell me what's bothering you?"

Nargis collected herself and then blurted out, "I saw Uncle Rana doing it with aunt Kranti in doggie fashion."

"When, where!" Shanti felt her blood turn cold.

"In the office-cum-library. I had come from school and wanted to tell aunt Kranti about my being chosen to play Portia in *The Merchant of Venice.*"

"Are you sure?" cried out Shanti.

"Yes, Mummy, I'm sure. I saw it with my own eyes."

"Were they naked?"

"Aunt Kranti's back was bare and Rana's trousers were down."

Shanti was still not certain as to what had transpired though she could expect any such act from her sister. She waited for several days for

Rana's phone call but none came. Again, he didn't contact her in any other manner, either through a letter or a visit.

Rana on his part knew that he had made a stupid blunder. He couldn't resist a few moments of foolish fun—with a tantalizing bare back in front. And this had now wrecked his marriage plans when he was falling in love with Shanti.

Shanti would definitely learn of it through Nargis. And she would never forgive him for this sexual indiscretion. In fact, he knew that Shanti had fallen out with Nari, her first husband, on the very score of infidelity. So there was no question of asking her forgiveness or making amends. As far as he was concerned, his hopes of marrying Shanti had now gone up in smoke. He didn't even have the courage to show her his face.

To Shanti, it was the ruin of a dream. Only once, after the failure of her marriage, she had harboured serious thought of a remarriage, and this had all come to nothing. The fiasco rattled her greatly.

A week later, Shanti brought up the subject of Rana with Kranti at breakfast. Nargis had already left for school. Drinking her coffee, Shanti suddenly snapped, "I hate you. I hate you more than anybody else."

"Why? What's the provocation this time?" Kranti knew exactly what led Shanti to make this hateful declaration, but had decided her only course of action was to minimize the event from her point of view.

"You know it. What you did with Rana in the library. You are a shameless slut. You could have easily taken someone else, not Rana."

"I'm really sorry. I had absolutely no intention to mess up your marriage plan. In fact, I'd like you to marry him."

"Then why did you do it?"

"Just from a sense of curiosity as to what Rana would be like in bed. In a weak moment I yielded to it. By the way, he's good." (Kranti would recollect that she had done the same with Nari before Shanti's marriage.)

"Shut up, don't talk filth. Indeed, I can't imagine a twin sister so debraved, so loose in morals. You don't deserve a place in this house."

Without a word, Kranti got up abruptly and left for her office. Shanti busied herself with household management, her mind numb, her future switched off.

28 Twins Come Closer, Then Sadly Part

Matters between the twins were sliding from bad to worse. It had come to a stage where they didn't want to see each other. Both took extra care to avoid a meeting or even talking on telephone. The parting of ways between the twin sisters appeared imminent.

At this juncture a terrible tragedy struck. Kranti was diagnosed as suffering from cancer of the uterus. Of late, she had been complaining of discomfort and pain. And she was not her usual active self. A biopsy confirmed the horrible fact that it was cancer.

When Bwana and Raminder learnt of it they made haste to cut their stay in London and return to Jaipur. Kranti sorely needed the comfort of Bwana's presence, besides his support in arranging medical treatment.

Overnight, the interaction between the two sisters stood transformed. Kranti had been stricken by a death-threatening disease. This brought out a swell of matronly feeling in Shanti. She took it as her foremost duty to comfort and nurse her stricken sister.

Dr. Adoor was contacted. He advised treatment at the Tata Cancer Institute, Bombay, and volunteered to go along with them. Bwana was keen to accompany Kranti to Bombay but had to admit that his physical disability would prove more of a hindrance than help.

The three travelled to Bombay. The doctors at the institute confirmed the diagnosis and advised an immediate removal of the affected uterus. They feared that any delay would spread the cancerous cells to other parts of the body.

"I'd prefer to be operated in New York," said Kranti. She had lived there and had heard of a famous research institute there, the Memorial Sloan-Kettering Cancer Centre. Dr. Adoor saw no harm in taking a chance at the famous facility. Bwana gave his full support to the proposal. Again he toyed with the idea of accompanying them to the USA but found it inadvisable in his physical condition. He, however, consoled himself with the fact that the twins were no longer fighting with each other. Indeed, Shanti was nursing her stricken twin sister more like a mother than an elder sister older by nine minutes. Bwana was keen that Kranti got the best available treatment.

Within no time, admission was secured in the New York hospital, travel documents obtained, and so also foreign exchange. Shanti accompanied Kranti to New York.

The doctors at the cancer hospital were rather unhappy that Kranti had come somewhat late. They feared that the infection could have spread beyond the uterus.

Kranti was operated on and her uterus removed. And as a precautionary measure she was put on a rigorous course of chemotherapy. The two sisters stayed in a hotel room close to the Cancer Centre, Shanti looking after her convalescent sister undergoing periodic checks and treatment at the hospital. They had to stay in New York for nearly three months. Kranti hated the weekly chemotherapy sessions. It reduced her appetite, made her lose much of her hair, and shrank her body. She would moan in desperation, "Why this uterus cancer?"

"Cancer can occur anywhere; breast cancer, uterus cancer, or any other cancer."

"Is it because I led a promiscuous life? I had quite a few sexual partners. God was punishing me for my licentious ways."

Shanti would rejoin, "I don't think God is bothered by such things."

Shanti brought her sister back to Devi House. Kranti had grown weak, lost a good deal of weight, and was mentally anguish. Further tests revealed that the cancer had infected the pelvic bone and spread to other parts, such as kidneys, even liver. Some expensive imported injections costing one and a half lakh each had to be given every week. They were so painful that Kranti would cry for hours. Even otherwise, her body was racked with pain all the time, with pain killers as her only relief. Dr. Adoor was a daily visitor but he again could render no help except words of sympathy and a choice of pain killers.

The doctors told Bwana that Kranti's cure stage had passed. We had only to take care and ease her life till it was over, they said. According to them, the end might come within months. Bwana would sit for hours with his ailing daughter, offering sympathy and support, with her shrunken hand held between his two large ones. Raminder, who was once annoyed with Kranti, was also extending sympathy and all possible help.

Shanti advocated the line that a last desperate chance may be taken through another visit to the New York hospital. This was also the expressed wish of Kranti. Dr. Adoor saw no advantage in going to New York at that stage. Bwana and Raminder discussed it for hours. Bwana particularly felt that but for some expense and travel fatigue there seemed no harm in making another attempt at cure. Raminder was also of the same view.

Shanti again took her ailing sister to New York. By this time, direct flights from Delhi to New York were available and so the travel in the business class was not so tiring. From Jaipur to Delhi, a nurse flew with them. At JFK airport, an ambulance had been arranged to take Kranti to the hospital.

Kranti got admitted into the same hospital. For four days, the hospital authorities ran a battery of tests. Yes, it was confirmed that the cancer had spread to the kidneys and liver. There was no question of doing any surgery.

On the fourth day, Dr. Heffner, the top oncologist treating Kranti, sent a message through the head nurse that he could be visiting her after the morning rounds. He also indicated that the attending Shanti should be present.

Dr. Heffner, a stately figure in his fifty, with premature grey hair and kindly blue eyes, pulled a chair and sat near Kranti's head. He grasped her bony right hand and said in a low tone, "I'm afraid its bad news for you."

Kranti stayed stunned with her head in her pillows. Tears were rolling down Shanti's cheeks and she had to look away so that the doctor did not notice this. Both these sisters had known that no cure was possible. Yet the doctor's words brought the stark tragedy home.

After a few moments, Kranti cried, "Doctor, how long will I live?"

"We can't be definite in these matters. But it could be something like three months." And Dr. Heffner got up to go. This was the big dilemma with oncologists that they had to communicate such terrible news to some patients and their kin. In fact, Dr. Heffner would say the same almost once every day. After the doctor had gone and Shanti had dried up her silent tears, Kranti spoke out, "The night Costa Rican nurse tells me Manhattan has one hospital especially for terminally ill cancer patients. Of course, nobody in the hospital goes out walking on his or her feet but they do take good care of the dying. Why don't you put me in that hospital and go home?"

"I'm not going home without you. If you have to be in that hospital, I'll take a hotel room nearby and stay with you most of the time. But I don't like this idea of your living in a place where everybody is dying. The two sisters kept quiet with their thoughts for a few moments. Then Shanti said, "Let's go back to Jaipur. Live in our beloved Devi House. Our dad and Raminder would be there and so also Dr. Adoor."

"Alright, let's go back to Devi House. I would prefer to die there than somewhere in a foreign land."

An ambulance had to be hired to get Kranti into the plane. And Dr. Adoor was there at Delhi Airport to receive and accompany them to Jaipur.

Back at Devi House, Dr. Adoor was a daily visitor. He often came accompanied by an oncologist. The main aim was to keep the patient as comfortable as possible, which meant a liberal use of pain killers. The question of any treatment did not arise at that stage.

Shanti nursed her ailing sister day and night.

"No use trying to nurse me," muttered Kranti, who had become a near skeleton. There were the protruding cheek bones, bony hands, and stalk-like legs. Kranti would say, "I'm dying."

"Till there is life, there is hope," consoled Shanti. "Who knows, a new cure may come about?"

"No, my end is near. You have been looking after me like a mother. You have always stood by me in time of trouble. Remember, how you helped me when I became pregnant."

"We are twin sisters. We'd surely help each other in trouble."

"But I have been so hostile to you for years. Please forgive all that, as I'll soon be gone."

"Don't talk like that. I have nothing but love for you. I keep remembering the happy days we spent together as girls. You'd always protect me when anybody bothered me. Do you recollect how we used to tease the nanny by hiding ourselves under beds or in almirahs?

One morning, when Kranti felt particularly enfeebled, she croaked to her sister, "I want to make a confession."

"Don't do it if it's painful." And Shanti made her sister sip a little water.

"No, I have to get it off my chest before I die," muttered Kranti with difficulty. "I had quick sex with Nari a few days before your marriage. Just did it on an impulse in a bathroom of the farm house at one of the lunch parties. It was more from curiosity than love for him. Please forgive me for that indiscretion," she mumbled in distress.

"I knew Nari couldn't resist women but this is news to me. Forget it. I forgive you." And Shanti propped a pillow under her ailing sister's head.

Kranti could only respond in a choking hoarse voice, "Thanks." Within a few minutes of silence, she sank back in the bed.

Later, that afternoon as Kranti lay cradled in the arms of Shanti, her breathing grew slower and then it stopped. It was all over. She had breathed her last.

The two sisters who started life together in the womb were again stood coupled at the death of one.

Instantly, Shanti ran up and woke her dad and Raminder at their mid-day nap. Adoor was also called in. The confirmation of Kranti's death was now a mere formality.

29 Shanti's Second Marriage

Within two months of the sexual escapade with Kranti in the library-cum-office room, Rana initiated feeble attempts to win back Shanti's favour. He had realized how narrowly he had missed marrying a beautiful woman from a rich family for a few minutes of fun. He had acted very stupidly in going along with Kranti's magic, in the process losing a wonderful match for a good time of few minutes—the most damaging some five minutes of his life. Shanti was in no mood to forgive him or to encourage him in any other way. For her, the Rana chapter stood closed for good.

For the last one year, Shanti had been associating a good deal with Dr. Adoor. He had been frequently called for help and advice by Bwana during the illness of Kranti, even when an oncologist and other specialists were treating Kranti. On most visits, Adoor would sit back after he had seen Kranti and talk over things with Bwana, Raminder, and Shanti. He was proving a pillar of strength in those stressful days. He had particularly come closer to Shanti when he accompanied the twin sisters to the Tata Cancer Institute.

In time, there developed much understanding and friendship between Shanti and Adoor, the same duly encouraged by Bwana. One evening, after a long chat between the two, Adoor had exclaimed, "Won't it be better if I'm with you all the time?" Shanti kept mum.

Adoor, taking a sip of lemon squash, went on to say, "You are lonely. You need company. And I'm feeling the same after being a confirmed bachelor for years."

Shanti conceded, "Yes, I feel lonely at times, though there is Nargis to give me company, and so also Dad and Raminder. On the other hand, you stay busy with your practice. And I suppose you have developed a lifestyle of your own."

Adoor put his hand on the hand of Shanti lying on the table, looked into her eyes, and said, "I propose marriage to you. Forget the past. Forget my brother. We are not the same." Shanti didn't withdraw her hand and said in a low voice, "This is so sudden, so novel. Give me time to think it over."

"Sure. Take your time. I'll be waiting for your response." And he left, stroking her cheek.

Shanti wasn't sure what to do. Her first marriage had been disastrous, and she was hesitant to plunge into another one. Even the Rana affair had misfired. On the other hand, Adoor was one of the most decent men she had come across; helpful, courteous, and wise. At fifty, he stayed handsome, erect, and pleasing. The most remarkable thing about him was his intelligent face and kindly eyes. The hairline had receded but he had retained a youthful appearance and a sprightly walk. His hands, a surgeon's hands, looked perfect in shape and fine in texture. Dr. Adoor was always well-dressed.

One evening after dinner, Shanti broached the subject with Bwana.

"Adoor wants to marry me. I'm not sure what to decide. I would go by your advice."

"I had my doubts when you wanted to marry Nari. But I have no such reservation about his elder brother. Adoor is a man of high character and gracious manners. You have my blessings if you want to marry him."

Raminder, who had joined the two by now, was also enthusiastic about the proposed match. She said, "Why should Shanti spend her life in loneliness? She would be happier with a loving partner. Adoor is a perfect gentleman. He'll keep her happy."

"Adoor is a confirmed bachelor, set in his own ways. How will he adjust to live with me?" mumbled Shanti.

"As far as I can make out, he is a very sensitive man and should keep your wishes in view. No wonder, he remains the best friend of Bwana," said Raminder.

By this time, realization had dawned on Shanti that her managerial role in Devi House was well-nigh over. Raminder was now the lady of the house, though it was not spelled out in so many words. This was one important factor that was impelling Shanti towards marriage. She wanted to be the lady of the house somewhere, even if it was an establishment less pretentious than that of Devi House. All this made her veer towards going in for marriage.

Nargis in her second year in college could not be relied upon to give a mature opinion, yet her views were important as she would be getting a new father, a stepfather.

One evening, after dinner, Shanti walked into the room of Nargis where the girl was sitting in bed, reading a book. Taking a seat nearby, Shanti enquired, "What are you reading?"

"This is the life story of Amrita Pritam, the Punjabi poetess. Mummy, you must read it. It's most interesting."

"Good. Give it to me as you finish." There elapsed a few moments of silence between the two.

"Adoor wants to marry me."

"Dr. Adoor!" Nargis exclaimd, "I thought he was just a friend of the family."

"Of late, he has been asking me for marriage. Papa and Rammi favour the match."

"Phew. I'll have two fathers, and both brothers. Isn't it a bit funny?"

"You are right. People could joke about it.

Nargis had a soft corner for her biological father, and she still entertained hope of a reunion between him and her mother. "Mama, think about it. Don't decide in a hurry."

"I have been thinking about it for more than three months. If I have to marry anybody, it would be Adoor."

"Have you talked to Nari about it?"

"No. That chapter is closed."

"Alright. Do as you like. I wish you happiness."

"You know, my work in running the Devi House is practically over with the coming of Rammi as the lady of the house. Time is now hanging heavy on my hands. Marriage to someone known appears a good option."

"Mama, It's for you to decide. I'm with you. But I do propose to continue taking an annual holiday in London with Nari"

"Yes. I have no objection to it. And I don't think Adoor will have any."

With the separation between Shanti and Nari, Nargis had the advantage of having only one superviser, her mother. With father and mother both there, you get two controllers. That way his present position was the best for her. On the other hand, being the daughter of a single parent has its own drawbacks. You envied people who had both parents. And by this time, she knew Dr. Adoor well. He was good natured and liberal in his views. All in all, her mother marrying him would be a help not a hindrance.

Despite encouragement from Bwana, Raminder, and Nargis, as well as pressure from Adoor, Shanti was taking her own time to decide. She wasn't sure whether there was love chemistry between her and Dr. Adoor.

One day, Shanti brought up the subject again with Raminder.

"I suggest you and Adoor spend a weekend together at some quiet, scenic place. You would come to know the love relationship better," suggested Raminder.

"This is rather a bold step. But I suppose it's worth it when such an important decision as marriage has to be taken. However, it's too delicate a subject for me to broach with Dr. Adoor."

Raminder responded enthusiastically, "I'll ask Dr. Adoor to arrange a nice weekend that offers privacy and comfort. You would just be a guest."

Shanti mulled over the proposal and indicated that she would go along.

Evidently goaded by Raminder, Dr. Adoor came up with the invitation that he and Shanti could spend a weekend together in a pleasant resort that ensured privacy and comfort. He had chosen a luxurious lodging in an old fort converted into a hotel. It was a place right in the countryside some 100 kilometers from Jaipur. As he drove her there in his Honda on a bright October afternoon, Dr. Adoor smilingly remarked, "Do you want separate rooms or a single one for both of us?"

"Surely, separate rooms," she said. Shanti was clear in her mind that the weekend outing would not go beyond holding hands, half embraces, at the most a kiss. Anything beyond that had to wait till the actual marriage.

"To ease your mind, I have booked two separate rooms."

This weekend outing was a resounding success. The rooms in the old fort were huge and lavishly furnished. The surrounding area for miles was yellow with mustard plants. After having settled in their rooms, they went for a walk in the fields hand in hand. Later, it was a glass of wine each and an excellent dinner, and then an hour or two sitting on the terrace under a full moon, sipping coffee and cognac. All this time, Adoor was holding her hand, even moving up his own hand to her elbow and above; the silky arm looking so inviting. On getting up to go, Adoor held her into a tight embrace, with Shanti trying to wriggle out, and he planted a fervent kiss on her lips. Shanti went along with it but didn't kiss in turn and walked out to her room. It came to Dr. Adoor a pleasant surprise that Shanti was not only very beautiful but retained a youngish body. They drove back next day after lunch.

The trip had made a deep impression on Shanti. Here was a man who was handsome, talented, helpful, and in love with her. He was entirely different from his younger brother. To Adoor, Shanti looked more winsome than ever.

One evening, when Dr. Adoor was visiting, he again broached the subject of marriage. Shanti nodded assent. Straightaway, Adoor got up and gave her a kiss, a light kiss on the lips. And then he continued, "Now that you have agreed to marry me, there's no rush up. Nari will be asked to sign the divorce papers. He would agree to it. I've talked to him about this matter. His only condition is that if Nargis is willing, she should continue to visit him once a year as before. On my own I told him that there will be no objection to it if Nargis is willing. The separation money will discontinue. But then we have money enough to lead a good life."

Adoor and Shanti got married on Christmas Day in a simple Hindu ceremony in a temple. It was a short ceremony with only a few relatives and friends present. This was followed by a registration before a magistrate who had agreed to be present at the temple. It was a marriage far different from Shanti's first one which had so many ceremonies and glitter. Nari was neither informed nor invited to the function as his presence would not be free from embarrassment.

Bwana gave Shanti a cheque for rupees two crore and Nargis a cheque for rupees one crore. Shanti was also asked to take whatever items of furniture, furnishing, and curios she wanted to take. By this time, she also had a hefty sum in her bank account from the separation money.

After a day, they left for Bali, Indonesia's famous tourist spot, for a week's honeymoon. They chose to stay in a cottage of a five-star hotel on the island itself. It was an idyllic seven days in sun and sand, swimming (both were good swimmers), choice food, and sessions of love-making between the two sex-starved people. Shanti's dormant sexuality experienced an awakening. Dr. Adoor, with the surgeon's delicate hands, was all consideration and care.

One day they visited the Bali mainland to see a Ramayana dance and drama, and motored up the hill amidst rice fields, small farms, and little temples. Here, Islam showed itself at its gracious best, allowing a full flowering of Hindu religion and rites.

Indonesia, a country with the highest Muslim population in the world, had retained a Hindu minority with its traditions of celebrating the epics of the Ramayana and Mahabharata.

Shanti moved to Adoor's house after the honeymoon. By now, the house had gained a few additions. There was a block of rooms at the gate where Adoor did consultation work, helped by an assistant. The house now boasted of a double garage and two servant quarters. Nargis chose to remain at Devi House itself. "Let my mother and Adoor have their private life. I'll stay with grandpa and Rammi, and keep my old rooms." She had full intention to visit Nari every year for a fortnight vacation.

To both Adoor and Shanti, it meant a union in their mature years. Adoor had been getting bored with his single living. Shanti had grown a far more mature as a marriage mate. There was every indication that this union would be blessed with love and happiness.

30 The Epilogue

To Bwana and Raminder, it promises to be a blissful life. They now live happily in Devi House. Raminder occupies the first floor suite adjoining Bwana's, though they share the same bed, an impressive doublebed recently installed in Bwana's suite.

Some say, one secret of happy marriage is separate bathrooms. Wives particularly like this arrangement as they can spread out their multiple items without risk of male interference. And they can take their own time there. This is the arrangement on which our hero and heroine operate. It's another matter that Raminder helps Bwana in his bathing. Hari, the valet, is no longer needed for it.

Nargis continues to keep the same set of rooms on the ground floor. She goes to the Maharaja College for her last year of graduation in economics. She is doing well both in studies and sports. Nargis has developed into a smart personality, with her mother's beautiful face and a thick crop of long hair. She appears to have her father's height that makes Nargis an inch taller than Shanti. Nargis is to join London School of Economics as she finishes her graduation. Nari has been helping her in gaining admission to LSE as well as securing her living accommodation in London.

Not only does Shanti visit Devi House quite often, she frequently talks to Nargis on phone. Nargis rarely visits her mother's place. She feels happy and relaxed at Devi House itself. The girl is shaping into an independent one with interests centred on studies, music (guitar), and sports (table tennis). A table for the purpose has been installed in the house.

Nargis was keen to have a fish pond in a corner of the compound. Bwana advised against it. "It would be hard to stop the poodles, the water dogs, from jumping into the pool and grabbing the fish."

It has now been left to Raminder to keep an eye on the girl. And Raminder does it in her own effective, unobtrusive manner. She already has the practice of bringing up Simran.

Both Bwana and Raminder are happy to have Nargis in the house. She is a cheerful girl and her presence enlivens the place.

You see Raminder with her face getting livelier and her body more sinuous. She has again taken to a morning ride. Between breakfast and lunch she is at the beauty parlour. The business has expanded with the addition of laser machine for removal of unwanted hair. This meant an investment of nearly rupees thirty lakh. The income from the beauty parlour has shot up with the introduction of the laser machine. For a full-body hair removal the charge is rupees one lakh or more. A female dermatologist is there at the clinic everyday during the morning hours.

In due course, Raminder also got hair on her legs removed by laser; she had no facial hair or hair on her arms and torso. Bwana is amazed at the smoothness of her thighs after the laser machine had done its periodic work over a period of six months. Whenever an opportunity offered, he would keep on sliding his hands over her silky thighs.

One day, Raminder asked Bwana as to what she should do with the flat that he had gifted to her.

"Sell it, and put the proceeds in your separate bank account."

"You gave it to me. You can have it back or sell it yourself."

"No, I gifted the flat to you. It's yours." And in due course he found a buyer for her. Both Simran and Nargis also sold their flats. Simran's husband has built a house of his own on a prime plot. Nargis has no early plan to live in her flat as she was going to London for higher education and an uncertain life thereafter.

In the early morning hours, Bwana is doing his exercises and the therapy session. After a late breakfast, he is in his library-cum-office till lunch. Presently, his main business is investments. At one time he worked hard to acquire money. Now it's money that works for him. He has taken steps to wind up Kranti's travel business because there is none in the family fit enough to take it over.

Both he and Raminder are focusing their energy and resources on women's welfare. A 50-room hostel has already come up for working women who have no other place to live. A member of his staff stands deputed to run the hostel, while Raminder plays a supervisory role.

After lunch, the two take rest, which means a nap. On some days, it also turns into love-play. Then, it is an hour in the swimming pool. An evening is there for social activities and visitors. Raminder is managing to run Devi House better than ever before. Her presence also makes social life at the place more cheery.

Bwana can't forget his loss of legs but he has regained much of his composure and friendliness. The city's gossip mills have fallen silent over them. Devi House is keeping its image of hospitality. Devi House's most frequent visitors are Shanti and Adoor, Simran and her husband. The latter's baby boy is often there to be with his grandma.

One evening, Adoor and Shanti are visiting Devi House. They find that Raminder is getting ready to go to her NGO meeting for welfare of widows, the Association of which she is the vice president. She persuades Shanti to go with her to the meeting. Indeed, she has been pressing Shanti to take more interest in this field of social work. Raminder and Shanti go off for the meeting while Bwana and Adoor sit down for a drink. "Someone has given me a few bottles of a Belgium bear, said to be the best in the world," says Bwana. "How about trying some this evening?"

"Sure, a good change from whisky."

Hari opens a bottle and fills two glasses. Taking a sip, Adoor exclaimed, "Execellent bear."

"You can take a couple of bottles with you." After a few moments of silence, Bwana continues, "Once we had framed a Wish List. I think it's time to make a formal will."

"What's the hurry? You are healthy and happy."

"I'm happy but not really healthy. I can't escape mental anguish over my disability. And I'm getting old. Can't you see a few grey hair?"

"Grey hair is better than no hair of mine."

"This time, the will would be much simpler," said Bwana. "Everything of mine goes to Raminder."

"Alright. Make a will if you so insist."

"By the way, my idea was to give the London house to Shanti.

Somehow, Raminder has developed a sentimental attachment to that house; the house where she got married and where she enjoyed a long honeymoon." Bwana didn't deem it fit to disclose that this was the house where they had the first kiss.

"Fair enough. You should keep the London house, more so as you go there every summer."

"Good. And I'm gifting the Delhi house to Shanti, gifting it straightaway, unconnected with the will. I understand the property prices for posh houses in Delhi are sky rocketing. Shanti can sell the house or keep it."

"Shanti will be happy to hear of it."

The two men are drinking the bear when the two women return. All the four adjourned to the dining table.

Bwana has become proficient in the use of wheelchair and crutches. Indeed, he feels that his legs are becoming a little stronger, though there is scant chance of his ever walking unaided. Bwana also misses the two white poodles that jumped upon him and slept in his room. Both of them died of old age. They have since been replaced by two white poodle pups. These have been house-trained by a professional trainer.

His friendship with Dr. Adoor is as close as ever. In fact, it is closer, with Adoor being his son-in-law. That's the difference between friends and spouses. Friends may undergo a cooling period but there's no such thing like formal separation or divorce as in married couples.

Bwana's life now stands enriched with his marriage. Every time he looks at Raminder, she comes to him as a pleasant surprise; the dimpled smile, the merry eyes, the sleek long hair and an alluring body.

It is now a blessed life for him. But blessings rarely come unmixed. He still finds the loss of legs not so easy to accept. To some extent, his life stands shrivelled. And the absence of Kranti is somewhat hard to forget. For some years, he had come in close contact with her and developed admiration for the way she functioned, as a daughter, as a business woman, and a practical solver of problems.

His business and financial side is doing well, and he looks forward to the years of happy married life with Raminder. He would like to forget the dull years; the past is another country, it can't be truly recovered.

Raminder is perfectly happy the way things are going. She loves to live with Bwana and likes living in Devi House. Simran is doing well and so also Rammi's brother in Ludhiana.

Yet she can't help nursing the regret that more than ten years of her relatively youthful period was spent in utter loneliness. The same sorry state would have continued but for her brazen sex initiative one evening, the same carried out with uncommon boldness and finesse.

Pity, Bwana had taken so much time to mull over his lost legs. Maybe, men are poor losers. She had to go out of her way to help him overcome this mental snag and doubts about his manliness.

Anyway, all this is now a thing of the past. She lives with a man she loves and enjoys comfort and security. She keeps a busy schedule with her business, social work, household management and active social life. And she hopes that the same will last many more years to come. Her life couldn't be happier than this. How long will this last! She can't help harbouring a foreboding that something could go wrong to this idyllic state. Rammi can't forget that afternoon which shattered her life, killing her dear husband and paralyzing her benefactor, followed by years of sorrow and loneliness. All she looks for is that no such curse be falls her again.

The life now lived by Bwana and Raminder is proving to be a real union of two lovers; lovers who had loved but stayed apart for years.

Index